Managers' Guide to Service Management

Managers' Guide to Service Management

Jenny Dugmore
Shirley Lacy

Business
Information

First published 1995

Second edition 1998

Third edition 2003

Fourth edition *(with updates)* 2004

BIP 0005

ISBN 0 580 42764 1

Typeset by Typobatics Ltd.

Printed by PIMS Digital

Contents

Foreword

The Authors and BSI Editor would like to thank the following organizations and their representatives for their support and assistance in the rewriting of this edition of the guide:

Aidan Lawes, itSMF

Don Page, Marval

John Groom, OGC

Lynda Cooper, Xansa

This guide has been developed to give unbiased advice on the management of services. It is intended for managers who are new to support services or who are faced with major change to their existing support facility. It will be of interest to anyone involved in the provision or management of services.

The guide is based on the knowledge and experience gained by experts working in the field. It takes the form of explanations, guidance and recommendations. It should not be quoted as if it were a specification or code of practice.

This guide can be used as a stand-alone publication; however, most readers will find it useful to extend their reading to other publications. The reader's attention is drawn to Annex D: Bibliography and other sources of information, which lists other publications, addresses and statutory regulations that apply in the UK.

The guide covers the *"why and what"* of service management, touching only briefly on *"who and how"*. Details on *"who and how"* should be obtained from documents listed in the bibliography.

Whilst every care has been taken in developing and compiling this guide the contributing organizations accept no liability for any loss or damage caused arising directly or indirectly, in connection with reliance on its content except to the extent that such liability may not be excluded in law.

The guide assumes that the execution of its recommendations is entrusted to appropriately qualified and experienced people.

Preface to the fourth edition

This edition was initially intended to be a re-print of the third edition with formatting changes to support a larger page size and consequent changes to table of contents and index. This re-formatting was aimed at improving the readability of this edition. The opportunity has also been taken to: clarify areas in Control processes and Release processes (Sections 8 and 9) and the Appendix on scoping; include some additional minor changes to the wording to improve the ease of reading; and to update the reference section. This edition is published under a new BSI reference BIP 0005.

1 Introduction

1.1 Why do we need this guide?

Organizations continue to require increasingly advanced facilities (at minimum cost) to meet their business needs. The increasingly cost conscious and competitive nature of organizations means that the quality and cost-effectiveness of services, and therefore of service management, are recognized as fundamental to an organization's success.

With an increasing dependence on support services and the diversity of technologies available, service providers can struggle to maintain high levels of customer service. Working reactively, they spend too little time planning, training, reviewing, investigating, and working with customers. The result is a failure to adopt structured, proactive working practices. Those same service providers are being asked for improved quality, lower costs, greater flexibility, and faster response to customers. This applies to both commercial and public sector organizations.

Effective service management delivers high levels of customer service and customer satisfaction: *but what is effective service management?*

Implementation of integrated service management processes provides control, greater efficiency and opportunities for improvement. Service management processes require service provider staff to be well organized and coordinated. Appropriate tools also ensure that the processes are effective and efficient.

The variety of terms used for the same process, and between processes and functional groups (and job titles), can make the subject of service management confusing to the new manager. Failure to understand the terminology can be a barrier to establishing effective processes.

This guide has been developed as a result of demand from commercial and public sector organizations. It is aimed at managers and staff responsible for implementing, maintaining, improving or procuring service management. It enables managers to understand the best practices, objectives, benefits and possible problems of service management. It recognizes that services and service management are essential to helping organizations generate revenue or be cost-effective.

This guide will be particularly useful to:

- Newly appointed managers responsible for support services;
- Existing managers who need to make or adapt to major changes;
- Staff who want an awareness of the management of support services;
- Those who wish to understand the requirements of BS 15000 in more depth;
- Staff who are contemplating a role as a service management practitioner;
- Those who are about to start a training course on service management;
- Customers who use services that may benefit from improved service management;
- Customers who have an interest in the service industry's view of best practices.

1.2 Using this guide

The individual processes described can be implemented in isolation, and each offers opportunities for improved service management. However, coordinated implementation of the full set of processes offers greater benefits. Often the output from one process forms an input to another. Too long a delay in implementing all components in some form can undermine those implemented already.

This guide and BS 15000 both draw a distinction between best practices processes and organizational form: a process is defined as a series of interrelated tasks to meet a goal. Service management best practices should be common to all service management activities, whereas organizational form varies from organization to organization, each organizational form providing a basis for best practice processes.

As the requirements for best practice service management processes are independent of organizational form, this guide and BS 15000 apply equally to large and small organizations. This is described in more detail in 4.1.

Service providers should adopt common terminology and a more consistent approach to service management, reducing the necessity to "reinvent the wheel". This guide gives a common basis for improvements in services. It also provides a framework for use by suppliers of service management tools.

The role of management in ensuring best practice processes are adopted and sustained is fundamental for any service provider. Initial adoption will not occur without management backing, nor will the quality of the service management processes be sustained without the continued commitment of management. Managers should also judge the appropriate level of documentation required to sustain service management: striking a balance between too little (leading to inconsistency in approach) and too much (leading to excessively bureaucratic processes).

The "Plan-Do-Check-Act" (PDCA) methodology included in BS 15000 and outlined in 2.1 should be adapted and improved as new or changed service management processes are implemented, or as the service changes. Ensuring that this happens is a particularly important management responsibility.

Implementing the advice in this guide, complying with BS 15000 or adopting ITIL®[1] best practices, should not stifle innovation or the organization's ability to respond to changing circumstances.

The following symbols have been used in this edition to identify different classification of text:

 Objective

 Benefits

 Possible problems

1.3 Background to the revisions

The later editions of this guide have been influenced by the practical experience of the early adopters of BS 15000, listed in Annex E. This group also provided feedback on the second edition of this guide and on *IT service management – Self-assessment workbook* (ref: PD 0015).

This edition now refers to the PDCA management system, which aligns it with ISO 9000 and the BS 15000 series and also reflects the growth in service management tools and the automation which has enabled rapid improvement in the effectiveness of service management processes.

[1]ITIL® is a registered trademark of OGC (the Office of Government Commerce), Rosebery Court, St Andrew's Business Park, Norwich, Norfolk, NR7 0HS.

1.4   Relationship to other publications

This guide can also be used in conjunction with the *IT Service Management – Self-assessment Workbook* (ref: PD 0015). This is a checklist that complements this guide. It has been designed to assist organizations to assess the extent to which their IT services conform to the specified requirements.

This guide complements publications such as the ISO 9000 family of standards and the TickIT guide.

This guide also serves as a management introduction to the detailed guidance in ITIL. The ITIL books offer expanded detail and guidance on the subjects addressed by this guide and BS 15000, supported by itSMF's *Pocket Guide and Dictionary of Service Management*.

1.5   BSI concordat with itSMF and OGC

Publication of this guide follows a concordat between BSI, itSMF and the Office of Government Commerce (OGC), as a basis for mutual cooperation and positioning of their respective publications on service management [i.e. this guide, BS 15000, the self-assessment workbook and OGC's ITIL].

In the concordat, all parties agree that it is important that industry should not be confused by the publication of two sets of documents from two different but authoritative sources and that their publications should align and cross-refer.

The intention is that both sets of publications form parts of the same logical structure. As a consequence the ITIL books and the BSI publications on service management have been integrated. This publication serves as a guide to the detail in the individual ITIL books on the subjects addressed within this guide.

1.6   Terms and definitions

For the purposes of this guide, the terms and definitions given in BS 15000 apply. Terms not defined in BS 15000 are used as their common dictionary definition. The reader is also referred to the terms and definitions in the ITIL books and the itSMF's *Dictionary of IT Service Management*. Details are given in *Annex D, Bibliography and other sources of information*.

2 Contents of this guide

This guide outlines the management system referred to as "Plan-Do-Check-Act" (PDCA) that spans all of service management. It also describes the best practices of the individual processes within the scope of service management.

2.1 Policies and framework for service management

Objective

To provide policies and a framework to enable the effective management and implementation of all IT services.

Effective IT services require policies and a framework for management of the organization, people, processes and technology.

A senior manager should have responsibility for service management. This responsible manager should be supported by a decision-making group with sufficient authority to define the objectives of service management as well as the policies and framework (frequently referred to as a management system) to achieve the objectives.

The decision-making group should also manage barriers to change, e.g. resistance to new processes. Barriers may be due to the organizational culture and staff or management attitudes. Influencing the culture of the organization requires leadership and clear and consistent policies, including a supportive personnel policy.

Following implementation of service management, subsequent service delivery and service improvements require the same senior management involvement.

For ongoing control, greater efficiency and continuous improvement the methodology known as "Plan-Do-Check-Act" (PDCA) can be applied.

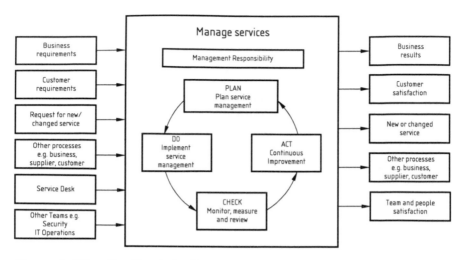

Figure 1: "Plan-Do-Check-Act" management system

Plan
Establish the objectives and processes necessary to deliver results in accordance with customer requirements and the organization's policies.
Do
Implement the processes and deliver the service.
Check
Monitor and measure processes and services against policies, objectives and requirements and report the results.
Act
Take actions to continually improve process performance.

2.2 Service management processes

> ### *Objective*
>
> **To deliver the agreed level of service at the agreed cost with the minimum overhead.**

Service management is composed of a number of closely related processes. The processes are grouped into five categories outlined in 2.2.1 to 2.2.5.

The model shown in Figure 2 also illustrates the processes within service management and within the scope of this publication. The planning and implementation of the processes should take into account the relationships between the processes. The relationships will depend on the organization and are generally too complex to cover in the generic model as shown here, and therefore relationships between processes are not shown.

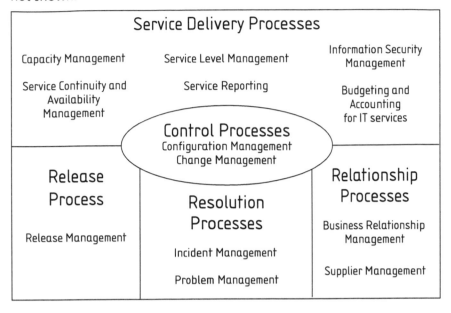

Figure 2: Service management processes

The processes are aimed at providing the best possible service to meet an organization's business needs within agreed resource levels, i.e. service that is professional, cost-effective and has minimal risk.

The processes can be applied with similar benefit to any service delivery operation, including non-IT service providers.

Benefits

- Improves resource utilization, productivity and demonstrable value for money.
- Makes the organization more competitive, reducing the risk, cost and time to market for new services and products.
- Improves value for money and service quality.
- Service provider is more responsive with services that are business led rather than technology driven.

7

- Projects work with the service provider to plan service management early, with better balancing of business benefits against risks to the services.

- More innovation and opportunity through technology-enabled change with the organization better prepared for major business and technology change.

- Provides a good understanding of the customer's requirements, concerns and business activities.

- Improves ability to deliver stable, higher quality, lower cost services with reliable support for business critical services.

- Resources available when required.

- Greater customer satisfaction with the service.

- Supports the development of a good long-term business relationship.

- Ability to manage suppliers effectively.

- Useful statistics enabling better decision-making.

- More stable work environment.

- Recognition of the value of staff, service and service management.

- Provides support staff with goals and an understanding of their customers' needs.

- Better utilized staff, improved motivation and lower staff turnover.

- Clear career structure and opportunity for career development.

2.2.1 Service delivery processes

Service delivery processes form the largest group. These are generally proactive, and are normally performed over long time-scales.

2.2.2 Relationship processes

Relationship processes are those that involve the interface between the service provider and the customer/business, and the service provider with any subcontracted third-party suppliers. The service provider might be an in-house service team or a third party where the service has been outsourced.

2.2.3   Resolution processes

Resolution processes are focused on incidents being resolved or prevented. Resolution processes are often centred on a service or help desk focused on dealing with incidents and problems.

2.2.4   Control processes

Control processes are focused on managing changes, assets and configurations. They help to reduce risk and prevent interruptions to services. They are therefore fundamental to the longer-term quality and cost-effectiveness of the service.

2.2.5   Release processes

Release processes cater for the roll-out of new or changed software and hardware and are strongly linked to control processes.

Possible problems

- Bureaucratic processes requiring a high headcount dedicated to service management.

- Failure to get staff commitment, lack of training in service management processes and staff expected to adopt service management roles which are contrary to their personalities or technical backgrounds.

- Symptoms are:

  - inconsistent processes (often accompanied by noticeable lack of commitment to the process from the responsible staff);

  - lack of understanding on what each process should deliver;

  - no real benefits to the cost of service or the quality of service arising from service management processes.

3   Planning and implementing service management

Service providers use service management to deliver higher quality services and to drive down the costs of the service.

When planning and implementing formal service management it is important to:

- Focus on business process and concerns, not function or technology;
- Develop well-defined and understood business objectives and service goals;
- Clearly define roles and responsibilities including third parties;
- Ensure all managers and staff understand and are committed to their roles;
- Define the benefits in a way that they can be measured and realized;
- Deliver benefits and meet targets on time and to budget at each stage.

The management team need to make decisions such as:

- How far should we go?
- Is the cost justified?
- What are the indicators of good performance?
- What are the risks of achieving our objectives?
- How do we compare ourselves to others?

They should also define the objectives that will help to drive effective planning and implementation. Examples of objectives include the following:

- To align services with needs of the business and enable change that maximizes benefits;
- To improve customer satisfaction and the quality of the services delivered;

- To provide more reliable services to support business critical services;

- To reduce the long-term cost of service provision.

Understanding the benefits that the business, the service provider, individuals and stakeholders will achieve from service management will help to manage expectations and potential resistance to change from all concerned.

3.1   Baselining

Quantifying the strengths and weakness of an existing service is a fundamental precursor to planning and implementation of service management, management of major changes and also to continuing service improvement. A thorough understanding of the current service and service management is commonly referred to as baselining.

Baselining can cover the quality of service, service management processes, workloads managed, customer satisfaction with the service and cost-effectiveness of both the service and service management processes.

It is essential that the relationship between agreed service levels, actual service levels, service costs and the customer's perception of the service quality is understood. It is also important to understand the effectiveness of the service management processes as well as the quality of the service and workloads, as all these are strongly linked.

Baselining can include tracking changes in service quality over time (e.g. has the service really got worse, or has it really got more expensive?). Also, if the service quality has changed, what else has changed? For example, service levels are linked to the workloads, support staff headcount and the extent of automation. A rise in support workloads, if not planned for in advance, will have an impact on the service levels within weeks or even days. Service levels might be sustained for a short time by the staff reacting by working much harder, but sooner or later customers will notice a degradation in the service, even if they are unaware of the cause.

It is advisable to baseline before and after major changes. Thus, for new or changed service management processes the cost benefit can be based on the impact of the processes on the baseline service levels and costs. Similarly, for major changes to the service, the cost benefit of the change can be measured as well as the impact on the customer's perception of the service.

When baselining involves comparison with other organizations it is usually referred to as benchmarking. This is described in 3.2.

3.2   Benchmarking

Benchmarking compares the services and service management processes of different organizations or different units within an organization.

An audit against the requirements of BS 15000 is also an example of benchmarking of the service management processes, as described in 3.3. Other benchmarking, such as the comparison of service quality, are limited by the need to compare organizations and services that are either the same or very similar. It is essential that the differences between a benchmarking group and the service being benchmarked is understood and quantified if the comparison is to provide useful information. Inappropriate comparisons in benchmarking can be dangerously misleading.

Benchmarking often reveals quick-win opportunities that are easy and low cost to implement, providing substantial benefits in process effectiveness, cost reduction, or staff synergy. Many organizations use benchmarking successfully and find that the costs of benchmarking are repaid through the benefits realized from acting on the information provided.

Some customers use benchmarking to decide whether they should change their service provider. The benchmark can be made against:

- A baseline set at a certain point in time for the same system or department (service targets can be used as a form of benchmark);

- Industry norms provided by an external organization;

- Direct comparisons with similar organizations;

- Other systems or departments within the same company.

Differences in benchmarking results between organizations are normal, should be understood and might be justified. All organizations and service provider infrastructures are unique and most are going through changes. There are also intangible but influential factors, which cannot easily be measured, e.g. growth rate, goodwill, image and culture.

Of the four types of benchmark listed above, the first is a normal part of service management.

The second and third involve comparisons with other organizations. Comparison against industry norms provides a common frame of reference, but can be misleading if the comparisons are used without an understanding of the differences that exist across a wide variety of organizations. The differences between organizations can be greater than the similarities, and comparison with a "typical" result might not be useful as a consequence.

Direct comparisons with other organizations are most effective if there is a sufficiently large group of organizations with similar characteristics. It is important to understand the size and nature of the business area, including the geographic distribution and the extent to which the service is used for business or time critical activities.

The culture of the customer population also has an influence: many support services are influenced by the extent to which customers will or will not accept restrictions on what they themselves may do with the technology provided. For example, it is difficult to have good security standards with customers who will not keep their passwords secure, or who load unlicensed or untested software.

Finally in the fourth type of benchmark, comparison with other groups in the same organization normally allows a detailed examination of the features being compared, so that it can be established if the comparison is of "like with like". However, it should be noted that some organizations are unusually diverse and have divisions that differ more than different organizations.

Typical benchmarks are similar or identical to common service targets or reports (see Annex A, Guidance on SLAs and Annex B, Service management reports).

They include:

- Calls/requests per period, i.e. hour, day, week;

- Call/request wait time;

- Incident/problem resolution time;

- First time fix rate;

- Remote fix rate;

- Incidents/problems solved per person;

- Changes made per person;

- Units of capacity supported per person;

- Customer satisfaction.

Most benchmarks include some financial measures, such as "cost per unit", and an assessment of cost-effectiveness is a common reason for benchmarking against other organizations. This is particularly so for organizations that have only limited historic information and who are therefore unable to use service or financial trends to measure objectively whether the service is getting better or worse.

3.3 BS 15000 audits

BS 15000 provides a standard for service management processes, where audit requirements are comparable across all organizations, as the requirements of BS 15000 are independent of organizational form, size or type of service. It is important to define the scope of service management in advance of assessing or auditing service management capability, particularly for benchmarking against BS 15000. Particular care should be taken in defining the boundaries of an assessment or audit in view of the complex structure of relationships that exist between different parties within the service management environment.

The scope should be agreed between the assessor or auditor and the organization in advance, e.g.:

- The geographic boundaries;
- The organizational boundaries;
- Those processes that require full assessment or audit and those which require the interfaces to be considered.

Further guidance on scoping and certification is given in *Annex C, Preparing for a BS 15000 audit.*

3.4 Planning service management

Objective

To plan the implementation and delivery of service management.

Planning is essential to service management as it includes the translation of strategic decisions into services. Implementation of strategic decisions may also require a major change to the service and therefore to the service management processes. Organizations may implement service management because there is to be a major change to the service. However, service management actually provides much of the knowledge required for making successful changes. Planning also reduces the risk, cost and time required for changes, and allows the business to take advantage of the new product or services earlier.

Major changes affect many, if not all, the services and systems used by a business. The changes often have to be done within a tight timetable, and it is not usually possible to stop *"business as usual"* activities.

Service management planning should cater for changes triggered by events such as:

- Business and technology change often implemented through programmes and projects;
- Service improvement;
- Infrastructure standardization;
- Changes to legislation;
- Regulatory changes, e.g. local tax rate changes;
- Deregulation or regulation of industries;
- Mergers and acquisitions.

There are advantages in using BS 15000 as a quality goal, starting at the early stages of service management planning, even if there is no intention to seek certification.

Staff responsible for service management should be involved from the earliest stage of planning for service management, or indeed of any major change to the service. The staff should assess and plan for the impact on any existing service management processes as well as existing services. Staff that are involved in this way will buy into the planned changes because they understand the benefits and how they personally will be affected.

Management should define the scope of service management in a service management plan. For example, the scope may be defined by organization, location or service. Management direction and documented responsibilities for reviewing, authorizing, communicating, implementing and maintaining the plans are also essential.

A good project management method should be used, to ensure that the objective and benefits of the project and of service management are achieved within time, cost and quality constraints. When planning the implementation of service management it may be appropriate to use either a single project or a programme of linked projects.

Planning which approach is most suitable should take into account the following:

- Business need for the new or changed service management processes;
- Customer's requirements;
- Existing capabilities (e.g. people, processes, information, technology);
- Risks associated with each type of approach;

- Timetable and nature of any changes to the service itself;

- Resources available;

- Technology or tools available;

- The impact on different stakeholders (e.g. sponsor, customers, development, testing, support, operations, champions, change agents, employees, suppliers);

- Other changes taking place.

Typical costs and resources that should be considered during planning are:

- Resources to implement new and changed processes and systems;

- Training of service provider staff involved;

- Software and hardware for databases, systems and tools;

- Creation and maintenance of accurate service management information;

- Secure storage for hardware, hard copy documentation and software libraries.

Service management planning should also cover:

- setting measurable targets for improvement;

- defining the requirements and design of new or changed service management processes, people, information and technology;

- the interfaces between processes and how the interfaces are to be coordinated;

- production or amendment of documentation;

- new or changed skills of those involved in service delivery;

- implementation of the new/changed service management processes;

- monitoring, measuring and reviewing the implementation of the service management processes and systems.

3.4.1 Organizational maturity

Some organizations find it difficult to establish service management and improve the service when the service organization is immature. There are several ways of determining the maturity of an organization.

NOTE References to methods of determining maturity are given in *Annex D, Bibliography and other sources of information.*

3.4.2 Phased approach to implementing service management

For most organizations only phased implementation is viable. Few organizations are prepared to take the risks of implementing service management as a single extensive change. Even fewer organizations are willing to fund this in a single financial year. Phasing is therefore not only required to reduce risk, but also for financial reasons.

All processes interrelate with other processes and in some cases there is total dependence, so that it is essential to consider the order of implementation. The objectives of implementation, identified in the implementation plan, can be used as the basis of this decision.

The need for "quick-wins" versus longer-term benefits will usually influence this decision. For many organizations the biggest "quick-wins" will be from implementing one of the resolution processes, e.g. incident management. Conversely, where an organization is facing a major change it may be more beneficial to introduce the control processes, e.g. change and configuration management.

Service providers may phase implementation according to external requirements, e.g. legislation or new customer policies. This may mean priority is given to a process such as security management. Organizations may need to be compliant with legislation by having a service management process that controls software licences.

Although a phased implementation is usually the best approach, services will be at risk if the implementation stretches over many years.

A long delay normally means that the latter part of the implementation is less well managed. Part of service management is then done badly or not at all and service management does not deliver the expected benefits. The processes implemented early may never become fully effective, e.g. asset management informally evolving out of change management and vice versa. Similarly, change management will be relatively ineffective and manually intensive if there is no configuration management. Resolution processes are fundamentally reactive if incident management is implemented without problem management.

Badly implemented processes cannot be automated effectively, so that investment in automation does not bring the benefits expected.

3.4.3 Practical success factors for service management planning

Key points which should be considered when developing plans are:

- An understanding of both the existing service levels and of the existing processes;

- The scope and effectiveness of the current automation and an understanding of what can be achieved by use of new or changed tools;

- The ways that people work together and their individual competencies, skills and behaviours;

- The organization's culture, how to manage barriers that may arise from that culture and the staff's attitude to changes of the type planned.

A practical implementation of service management should include:

- "Quick-wins" to demonstrate the benefits of service management;

- Starting with something simple and adopting a phased approach;

- Involving customers, especially those that have been critical of the service;

- Explaining the differences that will be seen by the customers;

- Involving third-party service providers;

- Explaining what is being done and why to everyone involved or affected;

- Educating staff and managers to become Service Managers.

NOTE Support staff are often cautious about changes: it is particularly important that they understand the benefits to overcome their resistance.

Possible problems

- Lack of understanding and commitment of senior management and staff may mean the plans are impractical to implement.

- A lack of understanding of the current services and service management capabilities may mean the plans will be of low quality and lack credibility.

- The planning phase is inadequate to the scale of the change so that implementation is by stealth rather than by properly planned and managed projects.

- Insufficient recognition of the scale of investment in automation results in error prone and expensive manual processes.

3.5   Implement service management and provide the services

Objective

To implement the service management plan and achieve the defined service objectives.

Normal management practices are required for implementing service management and successfully delivering programmes and projects. These include:

- Allocation of funds and budgets;

- Allocation of roles and responsibilities;

- Documenting and maintaining the policies, plans, procedures and definitions for each process or set of processes;

- Identification and management of risks to the service;

- Managing teams, e.g. recruiting and developing appropriate staff and managing staff continuity;

- Managing facilities and budget;

- Managing the teams, including service desk and operations;

- Reporting progress against the plans;

- Coordination of service management processes.

Benefits

- Improved business and innovation opportunities as the business can take advantage of new products, services and business change earlier.

- Reduced service outages, customer dissatisfaction and risk of damage to the business.

- Reduced risk, cost and time required implementing new products or services.

- Improved business efficiency.

- Greater customer satisfaction.

- More reliable services to support business critical services.

- Improved staff productivity and satisfaction.
- Cost reduction in service delivery or ability to do more with the same resources.
- Saves time and money.
- The service provider can demonstrate value for money.

3.5.1 There are no "silver bullets"

New or improved service management can represent major changes. Changing any process always carries some risk to the organization. To get benefits from the changes it is essential to allocate sufficient time and resource to the change. Service provider staff and customers may need to learn new practices. What is perhaps less clear but still important is the key role that management have in avoiding the *"silver bullet life cycle"*, where new processes or tools are introduced and abandoned at the first sign of difficulty.

Enthusiasm for a change is usually highest in the early stages, especially if staff and customers are aware of the reasons for the change and the benefits predicted from it. However, changes to service management involve a learning curve that may be unpopular in practice and the predicted speed of benefit delivery may have been too optimistic. As a consequence initial enthusiasm may decrease rapidly.

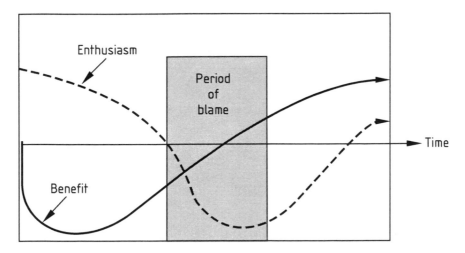

Figure 3: Introducing or changing service management

Until the change delivers benefits that outweigh the costs of the change the enthusiasm will be eroded. In reality there is often a stage where the costs outweigh the benefits; this shortfall is often linked to an even sharper fall in enthusiasm, as shown in Figure 3.

At this stage the organization may abandon the existing initiative, wasting the investment, and start the cycle again with an alternative initiative, without ever really understanding what went wrong previously and therefore facing the same cycle of events.

The role of management should be to encourage their staff to persevere and to work through the initial drop in enthusiasm, understanding and correcting any short-term issues rather than giving up. Eventually, as new processes or automation begin to deliver visible benefits, enthusiasm for the change will again rise. A successful outcome is possible if management remain committed to the change and display leadership during the difficult early stage.

Possible problems

- Organizations may not plan suitable phasing.

- Unrealistic expectations on what can be achieved may lead to a backlash against service management by disappointed staff, managers and customers.

- If new processes and best practices become ends in themselves, the focus on service quality and efficiency can be lost.

- Processes may be implemented without suitable automation, making processes inefficient and error prone.

- There may be no demonstrable improvement due to lack of understanding of what is achievable and how performance can be monitored and controlled.

3.6   Monitoring, measuring and reviewing

Objective

To monitor, measure and review whether the service management objectives and plan are being achieved.

The necessity of monitoring and reviewing the service is usually understood.

It is also essential to monitor and review the service management *processes*, as the cause of a low quality service may be inadequate service management processes.

Monitoring, measuring and analysis should encompass:

- Achievement against defined service targets;
- Customer satisfaction;
- Resource utilization;
- Organizational capabilities and competencies;
- Trends;
- Major nonconformities;
- Results of reviews.

Benefits

- Clear definition of how to measure a process and understanding of how to deliver the expected results.

- Ability to provide control based on the quality of the process as demonstrated from the results of each process.

- Knowledge and confidence that planned improvements are being implemented.

- Early warning of risks to successful service changes and improvement initiatives.

Benchmarking, assessments and local reviews by local management can all be used to identify shortfalls in skills, process and technology. There may be a periodic audit against BS 15000. The nature and scale of the processes should determine the type of review (or audit) performed against each process.

After a process change the scope of a review or audit should include processes linked to the changed process via an interface, as a change in one process may affect others. For example, changes to a release process may impact incident and problem management or change management.

A documented assessment of the shortfalls should be used for planning the next service and process improvements.

3.7   Continuous improvement

> ### Objective
>
> To improve the effectiveness and efficiency of service delivery and management.

Service providers should recognize the potential for making existing services and service management processes and associated systems more effective and efficient. As a consequence reviews are fundamental to continuous improvement.

All those involved need to be aware of their personal contribution to continuous improvement. Having a policy on continuous improvements and adopting a methodical and coordinated approach helps staff support the need for change in their role and in the service management processes. It will also help customers accept the implications to them and their service arising from the changes.

> ### Benefits
>
> - Taking little or no action at all normally means the situation will worsen, creating a crisis, which eventually costs more to correct. Continuous improvement therefore means staff function more effectively and prevents:
>   - staff being put under too much pressure;
>   - staff sickness and turnover increase.

Following the stages outlined in this guide and in the reference material listed will mean the processes and support technology are implemented well and are *"fine-tuned"* over time. Organizations will avoid the trap of only recognizing the need for improvements when a crisis means corrective action is required urgently.

It is also important for organizations to make sure improvements address fundamental causes and not just correct superficial symptoms. For example, if service levels have degraded due to an increase in workloads, superficial corrective action may be to recruit more staff to cope with the increased workload. This does not address the reason for the workload increase, which is the fundamental cause of the degradation in service levels. It is better to balance a short-term need for better service levels by increasing the number of staff for a limited period of time combined with longer-term proactive improvements that reduce the workloads. Another example is correcting perceived lack of control by implementing a different call logging. This is insufficient if the root cause is staff resistance to formal logging of their activities, or lack of training in how and why this should be done.

A positive staff attitude to changes encourages suggestions for other service improvements. This can be via suggestion schemes, quality circles, user groups and liaison meetings.

As described in 3.1 and 3.2, before implementing improvements both the service and service management processes should be baselined so that improvements can be measured. Improvement should be monitored against formally agreed objectives and compared to predicted improvement to assess the effectiveness of the change.

Improved automation, faster problem solving processes, problem prevention processes and a reduction in the scope of the service are just a few examples of corrective actions that may separately or together provide the desired overall correction. It is also often much easier to justify an increase in headcount (which is a fixed cost element of the service) if the increased headcount is linked to improvements in the efficiency of service delivery, such as those described above.

The choice of corrective actions can be strongly influenced by the funding available. For example, short-term funding may be available for improvements in support technology, if this is expected to reduce the fixed costs of support. Conversely, if the organization does not have the capital for support technology, so that automation is not a short-term option, it may prefer to restrict the services or take on additional staff until funding is available. Treating service improvement as a project with a finite time-scale is most common where specialist skills are required, or where the work will be so resource intensive that it needs funding beyond that allocated to routine service management.

3.8 Planning, designing and implementing new or changed services

Objective

To ensure that new services and changes to services will be deliverable and manageable at the right cost and service quality.

Proposals for new or changed services, including service closure, need to consider the cost, organizational, process, technical and commercial implications of the service change.

Planning and implementation should be based on realistic predictions of the budget required, as a badly implemented service will not bring the expected benefits and can place the service provider and customers in a worse position than before.

Plans for implementation of new or changed services should include details of:

- Budgets and time-scales;
- Changes to the nature of the technology supported;
- Details of any service closures (e.g. any being replaced by new services);
- New or changed contracts, service level agreements (SLAs), other targets or service commitments;
- Changes to service management processes, measures and support tools;
- The roles and responsibilities for implementing, operating and maintaining the new or changed service, including activities to be performed by customers and third-party suppliers;
- Skills and training requirements, e.g. technical support staff;
- Manpower and recruitment requirements, including any relocation;
- Service acceptance criteria;
- User training;
- How quantified benefits/outcomes of the changes will be measured;
- Communication to the relevant parties.

Benefits

- Services are properly designed and successfully implemented.
- Reduction in risk and impact to the existing services.
- Reduction in badly implemented services that do not bring the expected benefits and place the service provider and customers in a worse position than before.
- Better information on the total cost of ownership for each service.

- Actual cost benefits are reviewed and measured.

- Fewer projects finish early before the new or changed service is properly established.

The service will be at risk unless changes are done under formal change management. Not using the formal change management process for *some* changes to the service will also undermine the change management process itself. A post implementation review comparing actual benefits/outcomes against those planned is part of the change management process.

It is also important to have a process by which the new or changed services are accepted by the customer and service provider.

3.9 Impact of service changes on service management processes

A major change can mean many smaller changes have to be made at the same time so that more incidents occur, affecting the service levels provided. Also testing of changes, in addition to normal operational usage, could impact the availability and response times of the systems.

The established reporting mechanisms may be adequate for use during a major change programme, but this should be checked as part of the planning and any new or changed reports should be agreed and included in the deliverables from the programme.

It is essential that the cost implications of a major change are considered. Cost management and accounting practices provide a mechanism for predicting and tracking costs, and the expected cost of most major changes should have been included in budgets, in advance of the change.

With capacity management the capacity of a unit is known. The ability to do "what if" scenarios assists planning by checking whether there will be sufficient capacity for developing and testing during the major change programme.

The security implications of any programme need to be carefully considered. If security practices are already in place, then these can be used for the programme.

Continuity planning includes business impact analysis for major change. Business processes considered to be critical to the survival and success of the organization will be documented and form a start point for the planning. If a disaster recovery site is available, it may be possible to buy some spare capacity should that be required in the short term.

3.9.1 Relationship management

By having well established service levels and good relationships with the customers it is possible to discuss the effect of a major change and agree short-term amendments to service levels. As a minimum, customers will understand what is happening and therefore be more accepting of any disruption or inconvenience during the changes.

Many change programmes involve third-party suppliers. Having well established, commercially sound, working relationships with the third-party suppliers as part of service management makes agreeing necessary changes easier. However, it should be noted that there may be a need for changes to the service contract if suitable change control is not built into the existing contract. Contract renegotiation can involve time consuming negotiations and additional charges. It is *essential* that both be allowed for in the programme budget and timetable and started early in the programme.

3.9.2 Resolution processes

Good incident management processes are normally adequate for a change programme. However, additional resources may be required to cope with the increase in workload. It may be necessary to change the level and types of skills and the tools, e.g. new types of service report may be required.

Under some conditions (usually for a single large change, e.g. a new system being implemented) a prediction of the scale and type of support calls handled via incident management indicates that a short-term specialist support group may be a better option than expanding an existing help desk. This may involve short-term changes to support processes. This approach has the virtue of protecting the normal service delivered to customers not involved in the change programme.

This is a suitable option only if the *"who to contact when"* is unambiguous and the increased support demand is only for a finite period. Also, a short-term specialist support group may make it difficult to get an overall view of the service. It can also be difficult to close as the customers get used to having "their own" support group and resist its closure. Conversely, it is relatively easy to get a view of common incidents if the existing incident management is expanded to accommodate new workloads.

The problem management process applies equally well to management of incidents, events and problems from normal services and from major changes. It is even more important to have good problem management during major changes. The existing problem management systems should be used, although customization may be required to accommodate the new requirements and additional specialist staff.

3.9.3   Control processes

Major change programmes can affect all or most systems and services. It is essential to know what exists and what may be affected by the changes, before the changes are introduced.

Configuration management is even more important under these circumstances as the risk of making errors is generally larger than normal. Indeed, many companies find that by preparing for a major programme of changes they have identified many redundant pieces of software as well as being able to track assets more effectively. As a result they have saved money by removing redundant assets, capacity, licences and also reducing processing time.

Change management ensures that each request for change is handled in a controlled way and that the impact of each change is carefully assessed, costed and prioritized, taking into account all other current work.

3.9.4   Release process

For many changes effective release management and roll-out are also essential. Good processes and tools for software control and distribution ensure that updated versions of software are correctly and safely delivered to their destination, together with any platform upgrades.

3.9.5   Interfaces between service management processes

Failure to define the interfaces between the components of service management leads to gaps and overlaps, confusing staff and reducing effectiveness. This is not only a risk on initial implementation, but the risk is compounded during subsequent phases, because the established interfaces between processes and roles will change with the introduction of new processes. One of the major benefits of correct implementation is that roles, responsibilities and interfaces are defined and well understood. Gaps are also identified and can be filled.

4 Organizational and staffing considerations

4.1 Organizational structure

In this guide emphasis has been placed on processes instead of functional groups, the roles of individuals or organizational structures. Processes are the common denominator across all organizations. Although processes vary in the depth to which they are taken, and the skill with which they are performed in different organizations, best practice processes remain fundamentally unchanged whatever the size or nature of the organization or the roles allocated to individuals.

A process also remains unchanged whatever the name given to the group of people who perform the process. This is in contrast to organizational structures or functional groups, which do vary from one organization to another.

A source of confusion about the differences between a process and a functional group or organizational structure is illustrated by a process such as change management, which may be performed by a functional group also known as change management. Another example is where the change management process is performed by more than one group in an organization, albeit working closely together.

A third example is provided by incident management. In many organizations the group performing incident management may not be known as "Incident Management", e.g. call reception, logging, tracking, etc. By custom and practice this process is usually performed by an organizational group known as Help Desk or Service Desk. Unlike change management the group is not known by the name of its key process. Some organizations label the group who perform the Incident Management process as Service Desk, rather than Help Desk, to reflect the link with service management.

Service management processes have been implemented successfully in a variety of organizational forms. Organizational structures should take account of local conditions. The recommendations in this guide can be modified accordingly. However, it is important to maintain the spirit of the advice at all times. The common theme is that it is essential that each process has an owner who has the ultimate responsibility for the process.

In small organizations one person may own several processes. Conversely, a large organization is able to allocate individual processes to individual managers and groups composed of people with specialist skills with personalities that are a good match for the process. Some people are happier planning long-term, some are more motivated by the stimulus of resolving a crisis or a day-to-day workload that is relatively unpredictable. However, over-specialization also has its disadvantages, as specialization may be rapidly perceived as tedious and result in demotivation.

In practice management have to recognize the importance of motivation and avoidance of either over- or under-specialization and how the balance between the two can be achieved in their organization.

Although there is no universal best map of process onto organization, the balance can usually be improved by introducing variety into the roles of individuals, even when there are sufficient people to allow for extensive specialization.

Allocating appropriately mixed responsibilities can help keep the staff motivated. This also has the advantage of helping an organization deal with the peaks and troughs in activity that are characteristic of most services and of service management processes. Examples of this are combining reactive incident management processes with proactive problem management or combining configuration and change management. Mixed responsibilities also reduce the risks of dependence on key individuals.

Once established, service management processes can be validated through internal or external audit. Deficiencies (such as a mismatch of process and organizational structure) should be identified and resolved within resource constraints.

In order to achieve teams of staff with appropriate levels of competence the service provider should decide on the optimum mix of short-term and permanent recruits. The service provider should also decide on the optimum mix of new staff with the skills required and retraining of existing staff.

The optimization of short-term and permanent recruits is particularly important when the service provider is planning how to provide a service during and after major changes to the number and skills of the support staff.

Factors that should be considered when establishing the most suitable combination of approaches include:

- Short-term or long-term nature of new or changed competencies;

- Rate of change in the skills and competencies;

- Expected peaks and troughs in the workload and skills mix required, based on current and future technology, service management and service improvement planning;

- Availability of suitably competent staff;

- Staff turnover rates;

- Training plans.

4.2 Who are the right people for service management?

Objective

To ensure that service management personnel are competent to undertake their role.

Successful service management is heavily dependent on the people selected for the roles involved. Even if the processes reflect the best possible practices, the wrong person or a badly trained person can make the process ineffective.

An effective member or manager of a service management team is a person who has or develops an enthusiasm for customer service. Someone who is only motivated by an interest in the technology may be very unhappy with a role in service management, and an unhappy person is unlikely to be effective. In implementing service management it is therefore important to take personality characteristics into account when selecting staff.

Service management roles, responsibilities and competencies should be defined and maintained as job requirements change. When staff understand their role and how they contribute to the overall service and service management processes they are more likely to be motivated and effective than if they are left to operate in isolation.

Staff require appropriate education, training, skills, and experience, all involving good management and personnel practices. Skills may have to be refreshed as the processes change.

NOTE: A person who is appropriate for planning and initial implementation of a new process or a new service may not be suitable for the ongoing operation of that process: temperament, skills and career aspirations all playing a part in how well a person does each type of role.

4.2.1 Careers in service management

Service management is now recognized as an area of professional expertise. Services and service delivery are more likely to be formalized; support and assistance to customers (frequently known as "users") are much less likely to be ad hoc. The attitude to service management has changed as the service industry has matured and the importance of good management practices has become recognized.

Maintaining the services and infrastructure is much less of a back-room task and has gained in status to become comparable to analysis, programming and project management. Staff working in service management can now obtain and apply specialist skills and expertise. This is strongly reflected in the professional qualifications available and the training associated with those qualifications.

As a consequence staff are also more likely to remain and progress within service management rather than viewing it as a stepping-stone to other service provider jobs. This confidence in their professional skills and standards results in staff retention, higher staff morale and thus a better service to customers.

4.2.2 Qualifications

Two organizations offer formal qualifications, using the core ITIL publications as their syllabus. These organizations are:

- Information Systems Examination Board (ISEB), a wholly owned subsidiary of the British Computer Society (BCS);

- EXIN, a Netherlands-based independent examination body.

Both organizations are non-profit-making, preparing and administering the examinations but not delivering training themselves. They work closely together on ITIL examinations, under the auspices of an overall governing body that also includes representatives of OGC and itSMF, which ensures that the commonality and integrity of the qualifications is maintained globally. Each offers examinations globally, either directly or through local agents. EXIN is predominantly involved in offering non-English language versions of the exams.

Training organizations are accredited by one of the examination bodies to deliver courses leading to the exams. The appropriate examination institute should be contacted for information on accredited training organizations, availability of courses and examination dates.

Certificates awarded are as follows:

- Foundation certificate in service management
  This tests for an understanding of the ITIL principles, terms, concepts and disciplines of service management. It also gives delegates an appreciation of the benefits of implementing service management. Training courses are typically two and a half to three days duration. This certificate is awarded after success in a multiple-choice examination.

- Practitioner-level examinations and certificates
  These are aimed at those practising in one or more of the specific ITIL functions, e.g. incident management or configuration management. Courses typically last three days. Currently certificates are offered in single subjects, though combination certificates are under development at the time of writing. This certificate is awarded after success in a multiple-choice examination based on simulated work tasks carried out in a case study environment.

- Manager's certificate in IT Service Management
  This certificate is aimed at managers and tests an understanding of the ITIL philosophy, including the reasons for adopting ITIL best practices, the management implications involved, the costs and the benefits. This certificate is awarded after success in written examinations and in-course assessment. Training programmes are normally comprised of two five-day modules and an optional revision day.

The above qualifications are primarily focused upon the Service Support and Delivery volumes of ITIL, with further qualifications based upon other volumes under development. Apart from the Foundation certificate, entry to the exam is allowed only following the successful completion of the training programme.

4.2.3 Professional competence

While the certificates indicate a particular level of knowledge and understanding, they do not in themselves demonstrate that an individual is either competent at a particular level or indeed up-to-date in their knowledge and capabilities. It is useful to encourage staff to be members of professional bodies. Candidates are required to satisfy a range of entry criteria demonstrating current competence and commitment to a code of conduct and continuing professional development scheme.

The BCS has many professionals working in service management. It has developed an Industry Structure Model that provides a set of performance, training and development standards for information systems professionals, including service management. This model helps organizations and individuals identify staffing requirements, create job descriptions, assess the competence of staff and plan training.

The itSMF has launched a professional body, the Institute of IT Service Management, to which individuals can apply for membership.

5 Service delivery processes

Service delivery processes include the following:

- Service level management;
- Service reporting;
- Availability and service continuity management;
- Budgeting and accounting for IT services;
- Capacity management;
- Information security management.

5.1 Service level management

> **Objective**
>
> To define, agree, record, and manage levels of service.

5.1.1 Scope

Service level management (SLM) is a process that manages and improves agreed levels of service between two parties: the service provider and the receiver of the service, i.e. the customer. The service can be provided by an internal service department, an external facilities management company or a third-party supplier company.

The SLM process usually includes:

- Agreement of the service requirements and expected service workload characteristics;
- Measurement and reporting of the:

- service achieved;

- resource required;

- cost of the service.

- Coordination of other service management and support functions, including third-party suppliers;

- Cost management and the cost justification of expenditure on support services;

- Review of service and agreement of changes to the service, the associated costs, the workloads necessary to meet changed business needs or to resolve major problems with the service.

5.1.2   General

The customer is primarily concerned that its business can function properly. If, for example, the business function is a payroll department, the customer is mainly interested in its staff receiving correct payslips on time. The customer is unlikely to be interested in the components of the service (e.g. the network, the payroll application or printer) even though each may be an essential part of the delivery of the overall service.

The SLM process creates a management framework, which disciplines both the service provider and the customer. The process encourages both the service provider and the customer to develop an attitude whereby they have joint responsibility for the service.

Typically this generates:

- Understanding of the customer's business drivers;

- Acceptance of the benefits of early discussions of expected changes to workload volumes or the nature of the service;

- Constructive discussions on better ways of meeting the customer's needs.

The SLM process may be combined with other processes, and in a small organization this can also provide synergy with a process such as change management. Similarly, small customer organizations generally need less complex SLM process. However, when a wide range of complex services is necessary, SLM reduces the risk of the service not meeting exacting business needs. The SLM process makes it easier to change the service as the customer's business changes and can also improve the cost-effectiveness of the service, by including the cost of the service in the measurements.

> ## Benefits
>
> - For many organizations, an effective SLM process is a major competitive advantage to the customer's business activities.
>
> - Effective SLM means a supplier is more likely to retain existing customers and to attract new customers.
>
> - SLM encourages the customers to consider, document and define their real needs.
>
> - SLM generally makes the service provider more focused and accountable, in particular by providing essential management information from which sound business decisions can be made.
>
> - SLM means the service provider is able to meet the customer's business requirements.
>
> - There is better alignment of third-party supplier support with the services required.
>
> - Other benefits include:
>
>   - service targets, business priorities, impact and costs that are understood, documented and acted on;
>
>   - clearly defined customer and service provider responsibilities, with avoidance of misunderstandings between customers and service providers;
>
>   - clear definition of value for money from internal and external service providers;
>
>   - the quality of service provided is monitored and easily identified;
>
>   - a sound basis for comparisons, ensuring like-for-like assessments;
>
>   - a sound basis for service improvement or quality.

The SLM process is often mistakenly thought to benefit only larger organizations. For any organization where good customer care, staff and resource management and financial controls are required, SLM can provide a prime driving mechanism for effective services. However, small service provider organizations may not need to have staff dedicated to SLM.

Service reports required for SLM are described in 5.2.

5.1.3   Service catalogue

The service catalogue defines the full range of all services and targets provided by the service provider department. The service catalogue can be referenced by other documents, e.g. Service Level Agreements (SLAs), avoiding the same text or targets being duplicated many times over.

The service catalogue is a key document to set customer expectation and should be easily accessible and widely available to both customers and support staff. An intranet site is frequently used for this purpose. The service catalogue may reference information and documents in the quality system document. All the information should be regularly reviewed and adjusted according to customer and business needs.

Some service providers arrange the contents of the service catalogue and of the related documents differently, but the principle of holding this sort of information only once, managing it and making it widely available, should be followed whatever structure is adopted.

5.1.4   Service level agreements (SLAs)

SLAs are primarily used to describe details that are unique to a single service or single customer group. By documenting the full range of information once in the service catalogue or the quality manual, the service provider does not need to duplicate information in each separate SLA. The SLAs are able to focus on the specifics of the service defined and important detail is not lost in a mass of generic information.

The details in an SLA are all negotiated, agreed and documented as part of SLM. It is essential that the SLAs be formally authorized by both the customer's and service provider's senior management. The authorization should be handled in this way to ensure full understanding and senior management backing to the agreed service commitments.

The details may be held in either a single SLA or a series of SLAs. The choice depends on the scale and complexity of the services provided, geography and the number of the customer groups. The scope of an SLA can be from the very simple (*"all PC hardware failures will be corrected within x hours"*) to the extensive provision of a wide range of business services.

Supporting information on SLAs is given in Annex A. This includes a list of generic targets for SLAs, which can be used to prompt discussions on the planned SLA, but which should not be used without being tailored to meet local conditions. SLAs should include only an appropriate subset of the possible targets, as this focuses attention on the most important aspects of the service, avoiding confusion on what matters most and avoiding excessive overheads in SLM time and costs.

An overly complex SLA can be:

- An indication that the customer's real needs and priorities are not understood;

- The product of distrust of the supplier's ability to deliver a service that meets the customer's business needs, with the customer requesting many targets and supporting detail in the mistaken belief that it gives a greater guarantee of a high quality service.

The customer's views, business needs and perceptions should be the defining force for the SLA contents, structure and targets. The nature of the customer's business should shape an SLA. The targets against which the delivered service should be measured are those of the customer, not those of the service provider. A complex SLA may be simplified once the customer has developed greater trust in the supplier.

Continuity plan(s) and details of financial management are normally referenced from the SLA and not included in the SLA itself.

A glossary of terms is normally held in one place and is common to all documents, including the service catalogue. Even if terms are all those in common usage, it is useful to have a formal record of the algorithms for service level calculations.

As with other service management documents the SLA(s) are subject to change control. Where a change is significant, it is essential that the SLA be renegotiated and re-authorized. Information referenced from the SLA should also be under change control.

Major business changes (e.g. due to growth, business reorganizations and mergers, and changing customer requirements) may require service levels to be adjusted, redefined or even temporarily suspended. The SLM process should be flexible to accommodate these changes.

SLA(s) may also form part of a contract, in which case the commitments in the SLA(s) may, in the strict legal sense, be overruled by parts of the contract that have higher precedence. Typically, SLA(s) are a schedule in service contracts, and are as legally binding as the body of the contract but by being in a schedule have lower precedence. The lower precedence means that the commitments in the body of the contract overrule the schedules, wherever a conflict between the two parts of the contract arises.

Whatever the legal status of the SLAs, best practice service level management relies on SLA(s) as the definitive source of information on the agreed service.

For guidance on SLAs see Annex A.

5.1.5   Supporting service agreements/operational level agreements

Supporting service agreements are known under a number of different names, including operational level agreements (OLAs). They are used to underpin the support of the service levels agreed in the SLAs. OLAs are also known as *"back-to-back"* agreements. The OLAs define the services that *collectively* deliver the service described in the SLA(s) with the customer. Many of these services are invisible to the customer but contribute to the service that the customer actually receives.

They are similar to SLAs but instead of defining the aspects of the service key to the customers each significant component is described and allocated an internal target, e.g. print server availability, network up-time. Many of the targets listed in Annex A, even if not used in the SLAs, will be relevant to the OLAs.

The OLAs are critical to the SLAs, and a service provider should not agree an SLA without first understanding the service components as described in each OLA. For example, the SLA should not commit to swapping a customer's PC in two hours if the agreement with the third-party that provides the swapping service commits them to a four-hour target. If swapping the PC in less than two hours is fundamental to the customer's business (and funding is available for this level of service) the OLA should be renegotiated and the process by which PCs are swapped accelerated.

One of the main advantages of OLAs is that they clarify roles and responsibilities for service delivery groups and clarify supplier-customer relationships within the service provider's organization.

The service commitments of a third party are described in a full service contract, rather than in an OLA.

5.1.6   Service charters

Service charters are sometimes used to describe an organization's commitment to providing services. They are seen as a means of increasing customer satisfaction and retention. They may be similar to SLAs and if this is the case a charter or service guarantee could play a similar role in the SLM process, as the difference is merely one of terminology. However, some charters are informal or describe services qualitatively rather than quantitatively. Although this may be done with the best of intentions this type of charter is unlikely to be suitable as a focus for SLM, and will not bring the same benefits as an SLA. Charters can be useful as a high-level description of service commitments, and as a precursor to introducing a service catalogue or SLAs.

5.1.7   Third-party suppliers

Effective third-party supplier management is essential for effective service level management. Management of suppliers is covered in more detail in 6.2.

Possible problems

- The customer is required to learn the service provider's terminology in order to discuss service issues as the service provider has not attempted to understand the customer's business.

- Other possible problems are:

  - SLA(s) do not focus on critical business processes and are not regularly monitored or reviewed or are over-complicated and unmanageable;

  - the levels of service provided are not known or clearly understood so that SLAs are based on guesswork;

  - the levels of service being offered are unrealistic (e.g. they cannot be delivered with the current resources available);

  - no business cost justification exists for levels of service being requested, i.e. the SLA represents a customer's "wish list";

  - support staff and customers do not change working practices as SLM is introduced, invalidating the process itself.

5.2   Service reporting

Objective

To produce agreed, timely, reliable and accurate reports for informed decision-making and effective communication.

5.2.1 Scope

Service reporting encompasses all measurable aspects of the service, providing both current and historical analysis. It includes:

- Service reporting policy to meet identified needs and customer requirements;
- Developing and producing reports;
- Checking that the purpose and quality of service reports are effective and appropriate.

Service reports include:

- Reactive reports which show what has happened;
- Proactive reports, which give advance warning of significant events, thereby enabling preventative action to be taken (e.g. reports of impending breaches in SLAs);
- Forward scheduled reports showing planned activities.

5.2.2 General

The success of service management is heavily dependent on the monitoring, reporting and use of the information provided in service reports.

Effective reporting ensures that service managers can plan with confidence and deliver the service to the customer in a controlled manner, making best use of resources while continuously improving. Without reports to demonstrate service performance against targets and any relevant workloads, SLAs with the customer are meaningless.

It is important to consider the following:

- Whether the tools and techniques are cost-effective;
- How the production of service reports is to be funded;
- The savings that can be made in comparison to the costs of a baselining or benchmarking exercise.

Benefits

- Timely, reliable, clear, concise and meaningful reports for decision support.

- Effective operation of service level reviews by providing reliable data on service levels achieved and workloads handled.

- Proper documentation of tool usage.

5.2.3 Service reporting policy and requirements

Service reports should be timely, clear, reliable, and concise. They should be appropriate to the recipient's needs. It is essential that reports are objective and relevant to the interests of the target audience. It is usually advisable to have specialist reports with contents matched to specific interest groups, e.g. customers, managers or support specialists. Although each group may have similar interests, a single report should not be used for all readers.

Typical types of service reports that can be used in different circumstances are:

- Performance against service level targets;

- Non-compliance and issues (e.g. against the SLA, security breach);

- Workload characteristics (e.g. volume, resource utilization);

- Performance reporting following major events (e.g. major incidents and changes);

- Trend information.

Examples of service reports are shown in Annex B. It is important that these examples are not adopted without giving considerable thought to local circumstances and the specific business needs of both the customers and service provider.

The requirements for service reporting should be agreed and recorded for customers and internal management.

Where there are multiple service providers, suppliers and third-party suppliers, the reports should reflect the relationships between suppliers, e.g. a lead supplier should report on the whole of the service they provide, including any services by third-party suppliers that they manage as part of the customer's service.

5.2.4 Reports for customer management

Customer management should have reports that state the business impact/cost rather than charts showing trends in urgent problems. They typically include information such as:

- Problems with system x, delayed billing for y days, with loss of z;

- Power loss resulted in end users unable to work for x hours with costs to the business of y.

Customers should also have access to service management information, to help them manage their dependence on services, e.g.:

- Whether the number of calls handled by the incident management process are increasing and, if so, why;

- Which questions are most frequently asked;

- Decision-making on whether further training, education or user guides are needed;

- Whether changes (e.g. in data validation) would be effective in reducing support demand, and therefore the cost of the service, or increase user productivity.

5.2.5 Reports for service managers

Service managers should have tools and techniques for monitoring the service, reporting achievements and projecting service level trends. These help them to:

- Monitor and report actual service levels against agreed targets or objectives;

- Provide metrics on third-party supplier performance (external);

- Select related, or supporting measures of service levels in the light of:

  - tools/techniques;

  - non-compliance/escalation processes or procedures;

  - identification of service trends;

  - preventative actions or procedures.

Incident and problem management should have reactive and proactive reports to manage the service on a day-to-day basis. Decisions can then be made, for example, to:

- Invoke escalation procedures;

- Reallocate resources to best meet customer's needs;

- Improve user awareness and education.

All service managers should have reports so that they can manage the people, the processes and the components of the infrastructure for which they are responsible in order to maximize the benefits. The reports should help them to identify, e.g.:

- Service trends;

- Unreliable components of the infrastructure;

- Resource/cost intensive tasks.

5.2.6   Developing and producing service reports

Service reports should be timely, clear, reliable, and concise. They should be appropriate to the recipient's needs and of sufficient accuracy to be used as a decision support tool. The presentation should aid the understanding of the reports so that they are easy to assimilate, e.g. use of charts.

The following questions should be asked before designing or issuing a report:

- What does the recipient want to know and why?

- Are all required supporting metrics available?

- Are measures collected, analysed and reported with sufficient accuracy for the intended purpose?

- Are measures collected to an unnecessary degree of accuracy?

- Are measures being reported to a greater precision than the accuracy of monitoring justifies?

- Are measures presented in terms that are easily understood by the recipient?

- Who interprets the data?

- If algorithms are used are they easily understood when the report is interpreted?

- Is the frequency of the report appropriate?

- Do the reports stand up to the "so what" test? If not, the reports should not be produced as they do not provide useful information.

- Each service report should include its identity, a clear description, its purpose, intended audience and details of the data source.

Measures of the service in their raw format are rarely helpful and business critical information can go unnoticed in the mass of raw data. Intelligent interpretation of metrics, as well as their presentation, is essential if reports are to be effective. It is important to summarize and display reports in pictorial form so that they have an immediate visual impact.

The lead supplier should produce reports for customers and management covering:

- Performance against service level targets (e.g. outage and achievements);

- Non-compliance with standards;

- Workload characteristics and volume information (e.g. incidents, problems, changes and tasks, classification, location, customer, seasonal trends, mix of priorities and numbers of requests for help);

- Performance reporting following major events (e.g. change and releases);

- Trend information by period (e.g. day, week, month and period);

- Reports that include information from each process (e.g. the number of incidents and the most frequently asked questions, unreliable components of the infrastructure and resource/cost intensive tasks);

- Reports to highlight future and scheduled workloads.

Customers should receive informative reports at the right time in order that they can fully understand the resource/cost to service levels/business impact on service provision. The reports also enable them to determine, objectively, whether the service is cost-effective, achieves agreed targets, is within predicted workload levels and is responsive to the customer's changing business needs.

Management decisions and corrective actions should take into consideration the findings in service reports and these should be communicated to relevant parties.

Possible problems

- It is all too easy for reporting to become a mindless routine that ceases to add value but continues to add costs. To avoid this it is usually advisable to occasionally review the reports, adapting them as the readers' interests change.

- If changes are made, the continuity of trend information should be considered; it may be advisable to continue monitoring aspects of the service even if they are not reported regularly.

- Other possible problems are:

  - tools/techniques which are unable to measure SLAs;

  - need for complex manual intervention to produce reports;

  - "soft" (non-quantifiable but influencing) factors overlooked;

  - poor presentation targeted at the wrong audience and not understood;

  - reports delivered too late to be of use.

5.3 Availability and service continuity management

Objective

To ensure that agreed obligations to customers can be met in all circumstances from normal through to a major loss of service.

5.3.1 Scope

Availability and service continuity management processes together form a continuous process committed to delivering services without interruption and within budget. The two closely related processes have some differences.

Availability management identifies what can and cannot be controlled, dealing with and avoiding expected occurrences. SLM translates customer needs into SLA(s). Availability management then translates the SLA(s) into a plan for availability.

Service continuity management is concerned with the restoration of the service following an unexpected event.

It is essential that the two processes work together to give the right level of protection to the organization. Availability and service continuity are just part of the overall business continuity plan. In turn the business continuity plan should be viewed as a defining structure and major influence upon the development of plans and services.

Major service failures can occur for many reasons, e.g. denial of service attack, major virus outbreak, staff unable to gain access to the premises or a natural disaster. Many serious service failures are a consequence of actions external to the direct control of the service provider, but it is just as important to plan for these external risks as it is for those in the direct control of the service provider.

5.3.2 General

Organizations exist to provide goods or services to meet the requirements of their customers. The delivery of the products or services relies in turn on the continued delivery of supporting services. For most organizations IT is an essential support service for survival, therefore, an organization should ensure the continuation of services in any situation, foreseeable or not!

It is important to define availability and service continuity requirements as part of business plans, SLAs and risk assessments. Availability should be defined, measured, monitored and delivered in terms of the services required for the business processes, and in terms of the business user's access to the services it needs. Requirements for availability and service continuity should also cover details, e.g. access rights and response times as well as end-to-end availability of system components.

Changes to the requirements for availability and service continuity should be reflected in changes to the service or service management processes (agreed by change management) and in turn should be managed by the change management process.

Availability and service continuity plans should be developed and then maintained on a regular basis, with at least an annual review. If this is not done the business is at risk as a gap between the arrangements for availability and service continuity and the actual business widens as services, technology and other circumstances change over time. Service continuity plans should be tested on a regular basis due to this risk.

The availability and service continuity should cover all circumstances from normal through to a major loss of service. For example, it is clearly of little benefit to an organization, following a major fire at their head office, to have plans for the rapid reinstatement of PCs, networks and computing equipment when no plans exist for office accommodation for the staff, or if vital paper records have been lost. Yet this is not an unknown situation.

Loss of service should be monitored and recorded and unplanned non-availability, particularly serious loss of service, should be investigated and appropriate actions taken. Where possible, potential issues should be predicted and preventive action taken.

> ### Benefits
>
> - Services are designed and actively managed to meet specific availability targets required by the business and specified in SLAs.
>
> - Reduced downtime and maintenance costs means better quality services that are more cost-effective.
>
> - Availability of accurate historical information aiding the successful renegotiation of both SLAs and underpinning contracts.

An organization's definition of availability should conform to the customer's business requirement. The role of the service provider should be to aid business management in justifying investment in improved availability. This can be done by providing costs of downtime, business cases, etc.

Changes to the requirements for availability and service continuity should be reflected in changes to the service or service management processes (agreed by change management) and in turn should be managed by the change management process.

Availability management is a "back-office" process, usually performed out of sight of the customers. It involves dealing with how the services are assembled, delivered and supported. It is concerned with the effectiveness and efficiency of the service provider and its suppliers.

Even in a world of ever increasing hardware capacity and reliability, availability management remains an essential element of effective service management. Distributed environments mean that points of potential failure have increased some hundredfold, and so in many cases the increasing reliability of components is outweighed by the sheer complexity and interdependence inherent in modern business infrastructures. This complexity brings serious availability challenges and effective processes are required to meet these challenges.

Certain elements of service provision will always be beyond the control of management, and yet the customers will expect the service provider to deliver the service whatever the circumstances. Availability management sets out to ensure availability of all components of the service, and so should address, or work in harmony with:

- The underlying processes (e.g. backup and recovery);
- Scheduling;
- Security;
- Incident discovery and handling;
- Software and hardware maintenance;
- Change management;
- Local systems administration and customers.

Processes to ensure that required availability is maintained should include those parts of the service delivery under the control of the customer or suppliers. Neglect can undo the hard work carried out by the service provider.

Elements of availability include the following.

- **Availability:** the percentage of the agreed service hours for which the component or service is available.
- **Reliability:** the freedom from failure, and the ability to keep services and components in operation.
- **Maintainability:** the ability to restore services or components to normal operation.
- **Serviceability:** the support for which external suppliers can be contracted to provide for parts of the IT infrastructure.
- **Security:** the implementation of justifiable controls to ensure continued IT service within secure parameters (i.e. confidentiality, integrity and availability).

SLAs record the agreed availability requirements. However, the customer will consider a service to be unavailable whenever they cannot use it and a definition of availability should not be included unless it is in terms that are meaningful to the customer.

Improvement in one element will usually improve the overall availability. Similarly, improvements to maintenance and configurations that overcome failures or that provide alternative facilities in the event of a component failure (e.g. parallel networks) will all improve the availability. Traditionally focus has been on actual repair time, although in many cases better improvements to the availability will come from prevention and reduction in detection times.

Delivering high availability becomes more complex as processing power is transferred to the customer. It requires constant vigilance and awareness of both business plans and requirements and internal service provider procedures.

Change is the major threat to availability, and a temporary freeze on changes for a business critical period can provide the required availability with an acceptable constraint on flexibility. Other methods of influencing customer behaviour may be required. While these may be perceived as infringements on the freedom of the customer, many organizations will find it necessary to impose constraints to protect business critical services.

5.3.3   Service continuity management

It is essential that the service provider has a strategy that defines the general approach to meeting service continuity obligations, so that the process has a clear direction, and an understanding of any limits that apply to what is protected under service continuity, and what is not. This should be based on risk assessment of the various types of failure that could be prevented or minimized by service continuity, taking into account service hours and critical business periods.

The service provider should agree for each customer group and service the:

- Maximum acceptable continuous period of lost service;
- Maximum acceptable periods of degraded service;
- Acceptable degraded service levels during a period of service recovery.

The continuity strategy should be reviewed at agreed intervals, at least annually, to ensure that the business needs (or the threats to service continuity) have not changed without a parallel change in the strategy and plans. Any changes to the strategy should be formally agreed.

Service continuity management plans the full detail of restoration, with details (e.g. responsibilities and authorization for action) defined unambiguously.

The contingency management process includes:

- Initiation;
- Identification of requirements;

- Strategy (prevention or cure);
- Implementation of:
  - contingency management plans;
  - standby arrangements;
  - disaster avoidance/risk reduction measures;
  - operational management;
  - management involvement in contingency management.

The service provider should ensure that:

- Continuity plans take into account dependencies between service and system components;
- Service continuity plans and other documents required to support service continuity are recorded and maintained;
- Responsibility for invoking continuity plans is clearly assigned, and plans clearly allocate responsibility for taking action against each objective;
- Backups of data, documents and software, and any equipment and staff necessary for service restoration are quickly available following a major service failure or disaster;
- At least one copy of all service continuity documents should be stored and maintained at a secure remote location, together with any equipment that is necessary to enable its use;
- Staff understand their role in invoking and/or executing the plans; and are able to access service continuity documents.

Service continuity plans and related documents (e.g. contracts) should be linked to:

- The change management process;
- The configuration management process;
- The contract management process.

Service continuity plans and related documents (e.g. contracts) should be assessed for impact prior to system and service changes being approved, and prior to significant new or amended customer requirements being agreed.

Testing should be undertaken at a frequency and rigour sufficient to gain assurance that continuity plans are effective, and remain so in the face of changing systems, processes, personnel and business needs. Testing should be a joint involvement between customer and service provider based upon an agreed set of objectives. Test failures should be documented and reviewed to input to the service improvement plan.

Possible problems

- Difficulty in obtaining experienced staff and/or engendering correct attitude in staff.

- Difficulty in establishing the customer's business needs for availability and translating that into the internal measures to be taken.

- Lack of commitment amongst management, and difficulty in obtaining funding for a process, of which its crucial role is often not immediately obvious to those unfamiliar with it.

- Service continuity plans, contact lists and the configuration management database (CMDB) may not be available (usually due to a problem with the original plan) when a serious loss of service occurs, so that the service continuity plan does not in reality fully cater for the return to normal working.

5.4 Budgeting and accounting for IT services

Objective

To budget and account for the cost of service provision.

5.4.1 Scope

Accounting, costing, pricing/charging and production of budgets are all part of financial management.

Budgeting and accounting for services are part of service management, and should be performed by all organizations, whatever their other policies on financial management.

Pricing and charging for services are considered optional under BS 15000, but are outlined briefly in this section.

Responsibility for many financial decisions lies outside the scope of the service management arena and the requirements for what financial information is to be provided, in what form and at what frequencies may be determined without involvement of service managers. However, service management, and in particular SLM, should have policies on budgeting and accounting for services.

Service providers operating in a commercial environment may need to invest considerably more time and effort in their financial management compared to an in-house service provider. Conversely, for organizations where simple identification of costs is sufficient, the financial management may be much simpler.

5.4.2   General

The costs of providing the agreed services should be properly understood by both service provider and customer, for decision-making on changes and service improvements. Costs should include any charges from external third-party suppliers.

Effective cost management raises the profile of the true cost of service and makes it possible for the customer to judge whether value for money is being provided. Moreover, identifying costs and passing them on as charges also provides the service provider with the opportunity to qualify the demands made by the customer.

Customers are more likely to demand only those services that they *really* need if they have a good understanding of the costs of the services they have asked for. They are less likely to make unrealistic demands of the service provider when they understand the cost of the services, which they may have to pay for directly or indirectly.

In order to perform effective costing and accounting the main areas of expenditure should be identified and broken down into cost units, for example, staffing costs may be broken down into categories such as salary, taxes or training.

Each unit can be broken down further, for example, training could be broken down into specific courses. By combining data on the cost of specific courses with the number of staff attending each course it is possible to get a detailed picture of the cost of training.

Costs should be budgeted in sufficient detail to enable effective financial control and decision-making over the budget period. The budget figures become another service management target that should be met.

In order to manage to the budgeted figure the service provider should monitor and report costs against the budget, review the financial forecasts and manage costs accordingly. This is identical to most aspects of monitoring service levels and workloads within SLM. Changes to costs due to changes to services should be predicted and formally approved.

After implementation, changes to the costs should also be monitored, as for changes to the service.

Benefits

- Budgeting and accounting for services allows greater precision in the management of the cost efficiency of the service, leading to a reduction in the overall cost and/or the unit costs of the service, e.g. the unit cost of solving a problem (or the costs of avoiding problems).

- The addition of financial information to service options allows both the service provider and the customer to make business decisions on a more sound basis than where only service information is provided.

- Ensuring that the business provides sufficient funds to run the services it requires through the year.

- Early warning of under-use/overuse of shared resources.

Service management should have a clear understanding of the objectives to be met by budgeting and accounting, with the overriding objective of delivering cost-effective services without incurring excessive overheads.

Budgeting and accounting should be at a sufficient level of detail to allow:

- Cost types to be accounted for;

- Apportionment of overhead costs (e.g. flat rate, fixed percentage, or based on the size of the variable element);

- Granularity of the customer's business against which charges are levied (e.g. business unit as one unit, subdivided into department, or by locations);

- Rules governing the handling of variances against budgets (e.g. size of variance that will be escalated to senior management; links to service level management).

- Service managers should also understand how they do the following:

- Budgeting and accounting for all components including assets, shared resources, overheads, third-party supplied service, people, insurance and licences;

- Apportioning and allocating all indirect costs to relevant services;

- Effective financial control and authorization.

5.4.3 Accounting

Accounting processes should be used to track costs to an agreed level of detail over an agreed period of time. Accounts should demonstrate over and under-spending/recovery and should allow the reader to understand the costs of low service levels or loss of service.

Decisions about service provision should be based on cost-effectiveness comparisons. Cost models should be able to demonstrate the costs of service provision.

5.4.4 Budgets

Budgets are usually based on the costs incurred in previous years, taking into account any known changes to services during the budget period and, where budgetary requirements exceed available funds, planning for the management of shortfalls. Some organizations also budget for several years ahead as a separate exercise. The level of investment in budgeting and accounting processes should be based on the needs of both the customer and supplier for financial detail as defined in the policy.

Care should be taken in agreeing when the costs are incurred in the budget cycle. Budgets should assist in the process of managing costs by providing a breakdown in expected and actual costs for each component of the service at regular intervals during the budget year. It is normally useful to include:

- Current period (usually a month);

- Cumulative "year to date" figures;

- Rest of year forecast figures;

- Projected end of year budget figures.

Budgeting may take into account factors such as seasonal variations and short-term planned changes to service costs and charges. Cost tracking against the budget should provide early warning of variances against budgets, allowing action to be taken to correct the variance. Budgeting and cost tracking should support planning to operate and change the services so that service levels can be maintained throughout the year.

If the service provider is external to the organization costs, the budgeted costs are usually the third-party supplier's charges. The service provider's budgets include actual costs and the income arising from service charges, if these are levied.

5.4.5   Optional pricing and charging

BS 15000 does not require charging for services. However, many service providers charge for services and operate either as a profit centre or as a cost centre.

Internal service providers usually recover costs on a non-profit-making basis. The price charged to the individual customer or department may not relate directly to the service provider's costs. Organizations may opt for a charging regime where some services are knowingly under- or over-recovered, even if overall costs are fully recovered, e.g. pricing may be used for managing demand. This typically occurs where an organization has a long-term strategy to reduce costs by completely standardizing the technology used.

Organizations may also do this to keep the charging process simple, e.g. charges levied on a per PC basis are simpler than charging for the actual cost of the support work per PC or user.

Charging may also be the same throughout the year, but a service provider's costs generally go through a step change with the implementation of new technology, an extension in capacity or due to seasonal demand.

The impact of a charging policy should be taken into account when predicting workload characteristics. For example, if a pricing policy is that support charges for all types of PC will be the same, implementation of large numbers of new, high specification PCs with a wider range of software may generate additional support workload, but not additional income for the service provider. In this example, as with many others, the quality of service is likely to be directly affected by the pricing policy.

Some organizations opt for their internal service providers to operate as a profit centre. There are some similarities to the charging by third-party suppliers. However, although an external third-party supplier normally operates by adding a margin to the cost when calculating the charge, the margin (which may vary across different service lines or over time) is normally not disclosed to the customer unless the arrangement is that all costs are disclosed and an agreed margin is built into the agreement with the customer. The agreement of a fixed margin is usually referred to as "*open book*".

It is not normally necessary or productive to have the same level of rigour (and overhead) for an in-house service as is required for the accounts of a separate company, which is subject to formal auditing and legislation on accounting practices.

Whatever method is used for charging, it is essential that the method, the amount and the payment cycle and process are all understood before the service is taken on, and that proper provision has been made in the budgets.

Charges are normally raised retrospectively, usually on a monthly basis and in line with the budget cycle.

Possible problems

- If the budgeting and accounting for services becomes too lax, charges are not tracked or recovered, undermining the process.

- Conversely, the process may be too stringent and become an unproductive bureaucratic overhead. This occurs where charging is at a very detailed and complex level, or where costs are manually tracked and reported and the benefits of charging are outweighed by tracking, reporting, and recovering charges.

5.5   Capacity management

Objective

To ensure that the organization has, at all times, sufficient capacity, to meet the current and future agreed demands of the business.

5.5.1   Scope

Capacity management is a set of processes that ensures an organization's infrastructure has the appropriate capacity to meet the overall business needs, in a cost-effective way. *"Appropriate"* in this context means not too little, not too much, not too soon, and not too late. Excess capacity normally results in unjustifiable and excessive costs being passed on to the customer. Insufficient capacity usually leads to performance problems or failures which impact on the customer's ability to perform its normal business activities.

Capacity management is the focal point for all performance and capacity issues. The process should provide direct support to the development of new and changed services by providing sizing and modelling of services. There are three principal areas, as follows.

- Resource capacity management, which ensures that all finite infrastructure resources are monitored, measured, analysed and reported.

- Service capacity management, which focuses on managing the performance of the services used by the customers against the requirements in the SLAs.

- Business capacity management, which ensures that the future business requirements for services are considered, planned and implemented in a timely fashion. Future requirements will come from business plans outlining new services, improvements and growth in existing services, development plans, etc.

5.5.2   General

Capacity management ensures that an organization has the correct capacity relative to processing power, data storage, network bandwidth and connectivity, to meet and underpin its business requirements. It includes monitoring, reporting, performance tuning and the management of resources. Where appropriate, this involves influencing customer behaviour through demand management, e.g. via differential charging or specific controls on resource use. It requires a good understanding of the business demands, the resulting workload demands upon the infrastructure and the performance characteristics of each workload.

A key process in capacity management is the prediction of future needs. This ensures that any necessary procurements or upgrades are included in business and financial plans. It encompasses an evaluation of the impact of new or planned applications, systems or technologies on the existing infrastructure and upon the capacity plans. Gathering existing capacity data allows "what if" questions to be evaluated and, if necessary, modelled and calibrated to assist in the process of predicting future capacity needs.

Business predictions and workload estimates should be translated into specific requirements and documented. The result of variations in workload or environment should be predictable. Data on current and previous component and resource utilization at an appropriate level should be captured and analysed to support the process.

Methods, procedures and techniques should all be in place to monitor service capacity, tune service performance and provide adequate capacity. Service managers should make a judgement on the granularity of the processes in order to avoid collecting a mass of data that obscures the key points.

The service manager should assess the cost benefit of tracking the capacity of a specific aspect of the service against the cost of the tracking and the impact and cost of the capacity being under or over the required level.

Benefits

Effective capacity management reduces the risks of service failure, ensures cost-effective use of resources, and enables significantly improved planning and more informed and economic acquisition of resources.

5.5.3 Planning

A capacity plan, documenting the actual performance of the infrastructure and the expected requirements, should be produced at a suitable frequency (at least annually). It should take into account the rate of change in services and service volumes, information in the change management reports and customer business. It should document costed options for meeting the business requirements and recommend solutions to ensure achievement of the agreed service level targets as defined in the SLA. The technical infrastructure and its current and projected capabilities should be well understood.

Planning includes:

• Current and predicted capacity and performance requirements;

• Identified time-scales, thresholds and costs for service upgrades;

- Evaluation of effects of anticipated service upgrades, requests for change, new technologies and techniques on capacity;

- Predicted impact of external changes, e.g. legislative;

- Data and processes to enable predictive analysis.

Possible problems

- Unavailable, unreliable and inaccurate business forecasts and information with panic-buying at higher prices as a capacity issue arises.

- Customer expectations exceed technical capacity.

- Unrealistic and unachievable performance figures from equipment suppliers and manufacturers.

- Too much raw data for easy analysis of identification of features, as many tools can provide vast amounts of capacity data.

5.6 Information security management

Objective

To manage information security effectively within all service activities.

5.6.1 Scope

Information security is the result of a system of policies and procedures designed to identify, control and protect information and any equipment used in connection with its storage, transmission and processing. Security management is by its nature an umbrella process that requires awareness of the services and the full environment in which they function. The scope includes the implementation, control and maintenance of a security infrastructure. Arrangements that involve third-party access to information systems and services shall be based on a formal agreement that defines all necessary security requirements.

5.6.2 General

BS 7799 is the definitive standard on security management and its recommendations should be followed when implementing security management. Organizations certified to BS 7799 will satisfy the security requirements of BS 15000.

The risks associated with inadequate protection of these services are:

- Disclosure to unauthorized parties;

- Inaccuracy or incompleteness of information;

- Non-availability of information when it is required.

These risks are especially high when information is compromised without the knowledge of the owner or user, which is a particular concern with systems in which tampering or intrusion is not detectable.

Effective security management depends on accurate knowledge of the impact of risks and the costs of problem avoidance. Without them the tendency is either to ignore risks in the hope that they never happen, or expend disproportionate amounts on avoiding risks of minor potential impact.

Risks are an inevitable feature of life, but only manageable risks should be permitted. Security management is concerned with those activities that are required to *reduce* risks to manageable proportions, e.g. analysis of risks and definition of measures to reduce them. It also contains activities that are required to *maintain* the risks at manageable proportions, e.g. evaluation of effectiveness of measures, registration and trend analysis of security incidents.

Security management processes should ensure:

- All risks to service are identified;

- Manageable levels of risk are agreed;

- Procedures to achieve and maintain that manageable level are in place.

Benefits

- Business continuity and minimum business damage from security incidents.

- Compliance with relevant legislation.

- Benefits are hard to quantify, as views on the justified cost of security management are subjective and the benefits are largely the prevention of problems. However, it is usually possible to assign a cost to the actual occurrence of each identified risk and the benefit is the avoidance of that cost, e.g.:

  - costs of lost production;

  - replacement costs of stolen or damaged equipment;

  - compensation payments for unachieved contractual obligations.

- Estimating the costs requires business knowledge in order to produce financial values. It is more difficult to estimate costs for risks such as:

  - political embarrassment;

  - adverse publicity;

  - loss of customer confidence.

5.6.3 Policies

The legal and business issues surrounding a breach in security mean it is necessary for senior management to authorize an information security policy. It is also very important that policies (and any liabilities) are understood by the staff and customers, because security should be the concern of everyone. Information on security breaches should be reviewed periodically to ensure that the information security policy is meeting business needs, and if necessary it should be revised.

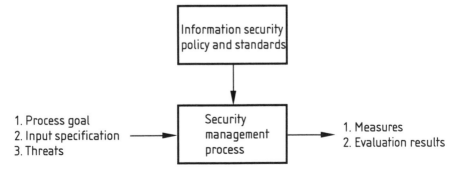

Figure 4: Overview of the security management process

5.6.4 Controls for security management

Security controls arising from the implementation of policies should be documented and understood. The impact of changes on controls should be assessed before changes are implemented. It is particularly important that security incidents are identified, reported and recorded as soon as possible. This is normally done using the incident management procedure in place to handle *"ordinary"* incidents. In many cases the person reporting the incident will not realize it is a security incident, as they experience it as a loss of service. It is essential that procedures identify security incidents and manage them in a way that recognizes the risks of a security breach and not just a loss of service. It is particularly important to be able to track types, volumes, cause and impact of security incidents for risk assessment and management of the service as a whole.

Guide to BS 7799 Risk Assessment (ref: PD 3002), provides useful guidance on risk management.

5.6.5 Virus control

One of the most common security risks arises from viruses, potentially causing a disaster in that the service may have to be closed down for an extended period of time. Even with a high standard of virus protection, a new virus can result in the service being closed down while it is isolated and eliminated.

All software and data should be protected from viruses. Information on virus protection and what to do if a customer finds a virus should be made available to all employees.

Procedures should be written to cover:

• The signs which indicate the occurrence of a virus;

• How to contain the damage caused by a virus;

• How to report a suspected virus;

• How to check floppy disks, tapes, e-mails and Internet downloads;

• How to receive regular virus protection updates and distribute these to all customers in a timely manner.

All external media should be checked for viruses before being loaded onto a network. Automatic virus detection software should be installed for critical systems, e.g. CMDB and secure libraries.

Localized problems can be encountered where a non-standard

technology is in place that does not give protection against existing viruses and a PC user either brings in an infected file or downloads something from the Internet.

Possible problems

- Some practitioners regard security as someone else's job, leading to an undisciplined and haphazard implementation of security measures. This can be further undermined by the view that *"it won't happen here"*.

- Security measures may not be designed and built into existing systems and services.

- To be performed well, this process requires staff fully conversant with the service who understand the full range of threats and risks which may arise. This range of skills is hard to gather and may require a team of people, bringing with it management challenges to coordinate the disparate skills necessary.

- Security management processes are generally unnoticed if they are performed well. The only exception is when proof of good security management processes is required for an organization to continue functioning, e.g. military or safety critical services. The low profile of security management can make it difficult to obtain adequate funding.

6   Relationship processes

Relationship processes describe the two related aspects of supplier management and business relationship management. Relationship processes include the role of a service provider, who logically fills a role between suppliers delivering goods or services to the service provider, and the customer who receives the services.

As Figure 5 shows, the service provider fills a role within a supply chain, where each link in the chain should be adding benefit, so that the services to the customer from the service provider are enhanced by the services or goods from the supplier.

Both the suppliers and customer may be internal or external to the service provider's organization. The figure shows a simplified representation of the relationships in a supply chain. External relationships will be formalized via a contract, internal ones by a service or operational level agreement.

In some cases supply chains are very simple, with no suppliers and only a single service provider. However, in practice, supply chains normally involve multiple suppliers and service providers delivering a complex set of interrelated services.

The business relationship processes should ensure that all parties:

- Understand and meet business needs;
- Understand capabilities and constraints;
- Understand responsibilities and obligations;
- Understand what customer satisfaction levels are appropriate;
- Ensure future business needs are communicated and understood.

The scope, roles and responsibilities of the business relationship and the supplier relationship should be defined and agreed. This should include the identification of the stakeholders, contacts and the lines and frequency of communication.

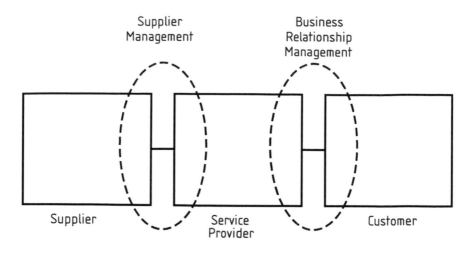

Figure 5: Example of relationship between service providers and suppliers

6.1 Business relationship management

> ### *Objective*
>
> **To establish and maintain a good relationship between the service provider and the customer, based on understanding the customer and their business drivers.**

6.1.1 Scope

The scope of business relationship management is the relationship between the service provider and the customer. This sub-section describes the processes mainly from the perspective of the service provider in their relationship with their customers. There are very close links between business relationship management and service level management (SLM) and many organizations use a service review meeting for both purposes. The relationship between service providers and suppliers is covered in 6.2.

6.1.2 General

One of the earliest lessons learned from implementing business relationship management is that the service provider's understanding of the customer's requirements or concerns greatly improves, and it will also learn a great deal more about its customer's business activities. Support staff, who have not previously thought of themselves as having customers because they themselves have little direct contact with the consumers of the service, understand who the customers are and the importance of the business relationship. It is beneficial for those involved in business relationship management to spend time actually working in the customer's own environment.

Service providers following good practices for business relationship management also understand the differences between customers (e.g. support services, even for standard packages, may need to be very different across different customer groups).

Customers who use a system for business and time critical activities need very high standards of service and may well be happy to pay the additional costs, as long as the service is seen to be providing value for money and is well managed. Conversely, customers who use the same system only occasionally, or use it for tasks they do not consider time critical or important, are unlikely to consider that high levels of service provide value for money.

Many organizations have people in both categories, with the majority of people falling into a *"middle of the road"* category. This mix of customers with a range of service needs can be one of the most complex circumstances to deal with and may only be finally understood when business relationship management is well established. Mutual understanding can be essential to high levels of customer satisfaction and a sound relationship between service provider and customer.

Failure to understand and cater for the range of needs across different customers, or customer departments, may mean that the *"average"* service provided is not adequate for some and too expensive for others. The result is that none of the customers are happy with the service. Effective management of the customer/service provider relationship recognizes and responds to the differences.

Business relationship management is also useful for understanding the difference between a business need and a *"business want"*, particularly where there are no service charges to help regulate requirements for new or changed services.

Benefits

One of the key benefits of business relationship management is that it generates a good customer–service provider

> relationship, based on a better understanding of the customer and its business drivers. This generates improved customer care attitudes and service levels. For the customer it increases its understanding of the role and scope of the service provider.

6.1.3 Service reviews

It is very important for the service provider to be aware of business needs and major changes, so that they can respond to these needs in a timely and efficient manner. In order to do this both service provider and customer should be in regular contact. This includes review meetings to discuss any changes to the business needs, service scope, workloads, SLA and contract (if present). It is also common practice for costs or charges to be considered as part of business relationship management.

The focus of service reviews should be on the customer's business needs, using the customer's terminology and jargon, not that of the service provider.

Management should make a judgement on the frequency of this review meeting, based on the rate of change of the service and the customer's business needs. It is good practice to have a review once a year as a minimum, while some organizations fine-tune the service on a much more frequent basis. The service provider and customer(s) should also hold reviews before and after major changes and, where appropriate, interim reviews to discuss progress, achievements and issues.

It is not possible to build a good long-term business relationship without a degree of formality. The normal disciplines of meeting management (e.g. producing an agenda in advance, effective chairing, minutes and action plans produced quickly) should be practiced or good business relationship management will not be achieved.

Actions for improvement identified by business relationship management should also be recorded and input to service improvement. It is very important that agreed actions actually happen, otherwise the credibility of the whole process is undermined.

6.1.4 Service complaints

Inevitably, even with an excellent service and a very good relationship between service provider and customer there may be complaints. It is essential that these are handled fast and effectively using an agreed complaints procedure. It is necessary for the procedure to include the definition of a complaint and how a complaint differs from an escalation. The service provider's contacts for complaints should be unambiguous to both service provider and customers.

It is particularly important for all complaints to be recorded by the service provider, investigated, acted upon, reported and formally closed. Where a complaint is not resolved through the normal channels and in the expected time-scale, escalation should be available to the customer.

It is advisable for the service providers periodically to analyse complaints to identify trends, report on this to customers via the business relationship process and provide input to a service improvement plan.

6.1.5   Customer satisfaction

Managing customer satisfaction with the service is a fundamental business relationship management function. Although every contact between customer and service provider can add to or detract from customer satisfaction, it is core to business relationship management.

Although objective reporting of costs, service levels, workloads handled and a high standard of SLM improves customer satisfaction, it should be noted that many customers base their assessment of the service on their subjective perception. Customers may not be aware of the actual service levels (or the supplier's commitments) or even the cost of the service to the customer.

Many customers consider service an emotive subject and may make unpredictable judgements even if they do know that the targets for response-time, fix-time or availability were achieved. For service contracts it is often the customer's perception that defines whether a contract is renewed, or whether additional services, equipment, or software are purchased. It is therefore important that customer expectations, perception and satisfaction are managed effectively.

Customer satisfaction may be measured by regular or ad hoc surveys. Although the surveys should be kept short and easy to complete, very useful information can be derived from satisfaction surveys. A survey that requires a long time or much effort to complete will be responded to by very few people, so that data is limited and may be unreliable. It is also essential, should a customer express serious concerns in the survey, for the service provider to be seen to address those concerns.

Although all those involved in service delivery and service management have an effect on customer satisfaction, it is strongly advised that the service provider has a named individual(s) who is responsible for monitoring, interpreting and managing customer satisfaction as part of the whole business relationship process.

Measurements of customer satisfaction are also an essential part of baselining and benchmarking. Surveys should be performed before and after major changes. It is also important to track changes in satisfaction over time, to identify both improvements and degradations. It is almost as important to understand why customer satisfaction has improved as to understand why it has degraded.

Monitoring levels of satisfaction will also give early warning of a gap developing between the services delivered (and defined in the SLA) and the business needs of the organization. This is common where the responsibility for the original SLA (or contract) is with a group who are unaware of the full range of the customer's business needs and how they have changed over time, or where the disparity of requirements across different groups of customers cannot be met by a standard "one size fits all" service.

The reliability of the survey is not simply a matter of sample size. Those surveyed should be truly representative of the organization as a whole to avoid under or over-representation. This requires the service provider to understand the customers and how they may differ from each other.

The results of customer satisfaction surveys should be discussed with the customer, an action plan agreed and input to the service improvement plan, with progress reported back to the customer.

Supplier staff should also be kept informed of the results of surveys and any action plans arising. This applies to both good and bad news, e.g. compliments about the service should be documented and reported to the service delivery team.

Possible problems

- Service reviews may lapse into "talking shops", producing no benefit. If the service review process is ineffective the customer will delegate attendance to junior management who do not have authority for decision-making.

- A common failing of customer satisfaction analysis is to compare "apples and pears" by comparing two organizations that have different cultures, business practices or different levels of funding for services.

- If those surveyed are not truly representative of the organization as a whole the survey results will be affected and perceived as unreliable.

6.2 Supplier management

Objective

To manage third-party suppliers to ensure the provision of seamless, quality services.

6.2.1 Scope

In supplier management processes the service provider is the customer of the supplier, and supplier management focuses on processes for managing the supplier. The supplier can be providing either services or products, or both.

Many of the features of business relationship management are present in supplier management, including reviews, action plans, service improvement programmes and good working relationships. A fundamental aspect of supplier management is the development and maintenance of formal agreements in order to:

- Describe the service to be provided by existing third-party suppliers;

- Use it as a contract for external third-party suppliers.

These agreements are often legally binding contracts between the service provider and the supplier. Whatever title is used, the common denominator for a successful agreement with a supplier is that it is formal and underpins the overall SLA with the customer.

Effective supplier management improves the quality and value for money of the service delivered. The third-party supplier is encouraged to find and implement improvements, be responsive to customer needs and is discouraged from becoming complacent.

The actual procurement of the supplier and supplier's service is not described here. The reader is referred to specialist publications on procurement. In the UK advice on supplier management is also available from the Chartered Institute of Purchasing and Supply (CIPS).

The role of third-party suppliers in providing part or all of an organization's services has grown rapidly, a trend that is expected to continue. In a BS 15000 audit it is the service provider who demonstrates conformity to these supplier management processes. The scope of the service being audited should be considered carefully and agreed with the auditor in advance.

6.2.2 General

The customer need not be aware that a part or all of the service is provided by a third party, as the service is seamless if controlled by a good service provider.

The requirements, scope, level of service and communication processes to be provided by the supplier(s) should be documented in SLAs or similar documents and agreed by all parties, as described in 6.1. Performance against the commitments should be monitored and reviewed, as for any other service commitment.

It is also important that the interfaces between processes used by each party are documented and agreed. In most organizations there are many groups providing each part of the overall service, with groups split across organizational boundaries and reporting lines. Service management processes include the management of the services from all contributors, irrespective of where they fit in, in organizational terms.

Supplier management should ensure that formal agreements reflect the potential need for change in the service, workloads or service levels during the term of the agreement, i.e. change control is included in the agreement. The agreements should be reviewed periodically to ensure that they still underpin customer SLAs. If this is not the case, or if a change requires it, the SLAs, internal agreements and third-party supplier contracts should be renegotiated.

Suppliers should be notified of changed requirements in a timely manner, as a service provider would expect to be notified by their customers. The timely management of requirements is particularly important with a long or complex supply chain. Understanding of third-party responsibilities, including changes to contracts, should also be made clear and communicated promptly.

6.2.3 Supply chain issue: supplier management role

The service provider should have documented supplier management processes and should name a contract manager responsible for each supplier. This should ensure that all roles and relationships between lead and subcontracted suppliers are clearly documented. Lead suppliers should also be able to demonstrate processes to ensure that subcontracted suppliers meet contractual requirements.

As with any service commitments, a process should be in place to review the contract or formal agreement, at least annually or as and when triggered by events agreed in advance, to ensure that business needs and contractual obligations are still aligned and the obligations are still being met.

It is also strongly recommended that a formal process is established in advance, as part of the contract, to deal with contractual disputes. Attempting to agree a resolution process in the middle of a dispute invariably adds to the scale of the dispute.

Similarly, a process should also be formally agreed to deal with the expected end of service, early end of the service or transfer of service to another party. For legally binding third-party contracts there is legislation on issues such as transfer of the service to another supplier, but the supplier and their customer (i.e. the service provider) may prefer to supplement these requirements with specific commitments and details.

It should be clear whether the service provider is dealing with all suppliers directly or a lead supplier taking responsibility for subcontract suppliers. The service provider (the supplier's customer) should also ensure that there is effective coordination of the suppliers, where there are several suppliers involved in each service.

Benefits

- A seamless service is delivered to the customer.

- Both parties obtain the best value from the relationship.

- Avoidance of uncertainty and minimizing risk by defining the role of third-party suppliers, the processes for managing the relationships and by managing them against agreed SLA targets.

- Reviews of ongoing activities of customer support and the methods of communication on a regular basis and instigation of corrective action.

6.2.4 Role of the supplier in service management

From the supplier's viewpoint good service and supplier management means that they have an unambiguous role and are judged on an objective and quantified basis, e.g. there are less problems from the supplier–customer interface, growth in workloads is managed and changes to the contract are amicable.

The key elements are therefore that the:

- Supplier understands the customer's requirements;
- Customer's requirements are met;
- Service levels are achieved;
- Changes are predictable and managed.

The supplier may be the group that actually initiates the best practice supplier management processes, especially when dealing with a customer who is relatively inexperienced in supplier management.

6.2.5 Contract management

Where the supplier is a separate organization, supplier management is usually focused by contracts that define the characteristics of the products or services provided. The customer may be part of a service management group, or belong to another area within the service provider's organization, such as finance, a procurement group, or be part of the business.

Contract schedules are often used to include service level and workload information. It is essential that the contract includes:

- A definition of services, roles and responsibilities;
- A definition of what will be done for, and provided to, the supplier;
- Contact points;
- Service level targets;
- Workloads (as bands within which service targets apply);
- Change controls;
- Authorization levels;
- Payment terms.

The contract may need to reflect the interdependence of internal and external suppliers and the responsibilities of the eventual business customer. Contract management processes should be agreed as part of the contract negotiation.

If the contract includes either penalties or bonuses, the basis of these should be completely unambiguous. These, and the rules surrounding changes to the contract, should be considered carefully as they can easily become a restriction, and handicap change, rather than a benefit. In general any contract that is very much in favour of one party carries a high risk of failing or being terminated early and at short notice.

The customer should appoint a manager responsible for contracts and agreements with suppliers. Where a number of staff are engaged in this task, there should be a common process to ensure that information on supplier performance is observed and acted on.

There should be a defined contact within the service provider responsible for the relationship with each supplier. A list of contact points within the respective organizations should be maintained.

In general good service management processes avoid serious conflicts between the supplier and the customer, as the unexpected does not become a problem and a problem does not become a crisis. Regular meetings, clearly defined roles and responsibilities all benefit internal and external suppliers alike.

The customer should judge the benefits of the contracted service: business needs may be better understood as a result of the contract negotiation and agreement.

After agreement both supplier and customer should review their objective in signing a contract at appropriate intervals, and where necessary agree contract changes. It is particularly important that the customer review their business objective in sourcing a service from a third-party supplier and take into account any changes to business needs since the service was first negotiated.

Negotiation skills, financial knowledge and an understanding of at least basic contract law are particularly important for supplier management of external organizations.

6.2.6   Selective sourcing

The majority of organizations depends on a mixture of internal service providers and external suppliers contributing to the overall service. This allows an organization to select *best of breed* services. They may choose to retain staff with specific business or technical skill, while sourcing other services from an external supplier.

It is essential that service management integrate each service, particularly when a relationship is being established with a new supplier. Particular care should be taken to define the roles, responsibilities and interfaces.

The organization should also decide whether it will manage each supplier directly or have a lead supplier. Both approaches have strengths and weaknesses. Both require skills in supplier and contract management. If these skills are not already available they should be developed before the contract is signed.

Possible problems

- The importance of supplier management is often neglected or delegated to a junior manager with technical skills but without supplier management skills.

- There is poor definition of what is being sourced from the supplier and why that supplier was selected, combined with a degree of abdication of responsibilities, rather than delegation, on the part of the service provider.

- Many business managers instigate and directly control sourcing from an external supplier, and underestimate the importance of involving their own internal service provider, who may have to work with an external supplier on an ill-defined basis.

- *"Show-stoppers"*, e.g. technical conflicts or inadequate capacity, may not be recognized until it is too late for cost-effective correction.

- Many managers manage third parties with insufficient involvement of the customer because they have neglected business relationship management.

7 Resolution processes

In any walk of life, when we have difficulties, complaints or questions, we want answers quickly and, more importantly, we want our problem solved. There is nothing more frustrating than making an enquiry to an enterprise or department and being passed around until you find the right person to speak to and possibly, even then, not having your request managed properly or resolved.

Incident management aims to restore the service to the users. It works with problem management, which is concerned with identifying and removing the causes of incidents. When handling many incidents at the same time, priorities should be set. These priorities are based on the urgency and impact of the incident on the business and the user. The priority for allocating resources to resolve an incident should also consider other relevant factors, e.g. availability of resources.

Wherever possible, the customer should be provided with the means to continue business, even with a degraded service, e.g. by disabling a faulty feature. The effect is to minimize the impact of the problem on the customer's business activities. This provides more time for support staff to investigate and devise permanent corrective action and to do this using formal change management.

When the cause of a problem remains undiagnosed but a method of circumventing it is established, details should be recorded for use during continuing problem diagnosis, or for use if a similar problem recurs. Where appropriate, problem management should develop and maintain workarounds to enable incident management to help service restoration by users or staff. Information on workarounds should be maintained in a knowledge base.

When the problem management investigation has identified the root cause of an incident and a method of resolving the incident, the problem should be classified as a known error. Known errors should only be closed where a corrective change has been successfully applied, or where the error is no longer applicable, e.g. because the service is no longer used.

7.1   Incident management

> ### Objective
>
> To restore normal service as soon as possible in order to minimize business disruption.

7.1.1   Scope of incident management

Incident management is both a proactive and reactive process and should respond to incidents that affect, or potentially could affect, the service. Its focus is on restoring customer service, not on determining the cause of incidents.

The incident management process potentially covers the management of all *"inbound communications"* as items of work. Communications may be presented as telephone calls, voice mails, visits, letters, faxes, e-mails, or may be recorded directly by users with access to the incident recording system, or by automatic monitoring software. The process includes the translation of a communication (which for simplicity will be referred to as an "incident") into a documented support requirement that allows relevant information to be retrieved and analysed.

The incident management process includes the following:

- Call reception, recording, priority assignment, classification;
- First line resolution or referral;
- Consideration of security issues;
- Incident tracking and lifecycle management;
- Incident verification and closure;
- First line customer liaison;
- Escalation;
- Major incident handling.

Incidents or identified problems that cannot be solved immediately are passed to the problem management process for identification of the underlying cause of the incident and its resolution. Analysing the incident management workload is important in order to identify areas for improvement, more effective resource usage, cost-reduction and customer satisfaction. Annex B lists possible report types.

7.1.2 General

For many customers the incident management process is the most visible of all service management processes. Incident management influences customer perception (and therefore customer satisfaction). It is important that this informal marketing aspect of incident management is taken into account when the incident management process is designed and implemented. It is also important that the incident management process is followed consistently. Deviations from the normal process are often noticed and can annoy the customers. The process is fundamental to representing the interests of the customers on reactive issues to service management staff.

Providing an incident management process greatly benefits any size of enterprise, supporting any size of customer population. The benefits of providing customer focused support are the same whatever the size of the group responsible for incident management process.

Benefits

- Improves customer convenience and satisfaction; requests are not lost, forgotten or ignored.

- Consistent management of customers and issues.

- More timely resolution of incidents reduces business impact and costs.

- Improves response, teamwork, communication and resource management.

- Improves control over third parties and suppliers.

- Essential, business focused, management information.

- Improved management of performance against service levels and targets.

- Less disruption to customers, users and support staff.

To meet customer and business objectives it is important to have a single point of contact for handling customer's incidents and complaints, e.g. a Service Desk. The point of contact may not actually be a single physical group in one location. Some organizations have a single logical group with distributed staff, performing an identical and coordinated incident management process. BS 15000 does not specify which organizational unit owns or performs incident management, requirements of best practice being independent of organizational form. However, in most organizations a Service Desk is the owner of all incidents and is responsible for progress monitoring. In this case the Service Desk should inform the users about the status of their incidents. All actions should be recorded on the incident record.

All incidents should be logged immediately. Classifying incidents helps staff to route the incident to the right resolver group and also facilitates better monitoring and reporting.

Several short lists should be used for classification rather than one long list that tries to combine several aspects, e.g. type, support group and origin. Typical ways of classifying incidents are: category (on the basis of the suspected origin), priority, affected service or support group. As the incident is progressed the workflow is tracked by using states, e.g. raised, accepted, assigned, resolved, closed. This is an efficient way of processing and tracking incidents.

To ensure that incidents can be resolved and closed as quickly as possible incident management staff should have access to an up-to-date CMDB and knowledge base. The knowledge base should hold information on technical specialists, previous incidents, related problems and known errors, workarounds and checklists that will help in restoring the service to the business.

Final closure of an incident should only take place when the initiating user has been given the opportunity to confirm that the incident is now resolved and service restored.

During closure the final category, priority, affected service and support group are checked and if necessary, updated.

It is also important to update the data on the component that caused the incident so that configuration management has accurate information on the quality of components.

7.1.3   Major incident handling

The profile of major incidents depends on the same basic incident management process, but there may need to be more resource and more management involvement. Major incidents may involve separate aspects of the incident being resolved by different groups, sometimes in different locations.

The interdependence of the incident and problem management activities puts the problem management process under pressure. The process benefits from nominating a responsible manager with authority over all groups involved in resolution. This person is usually responsible for ensuring that each group is aware of the activities of the others and that there is effective communication and escalation. This person also usually holds a major incident review after the service has been returned to normal.

Possible problems

- No visible management or staff commitment.

- Lack of clarity about business needs.

- Working practices not being reviewed or changed.

- Service delivery culture is not customer-focused.

- Poorly defined service objectives, goals and responsibilities.

- No provision of agreed customer service levels.

- Benefits and achievements not being sold to the business and customers.

7.2 Problem management

Objective

To minimize disruption to the business by proactive identification and analysis of the cause of service incidents and by managing problems to closure.

7.2.1 Scope of problem management

Problem management identifies and manages the underlying causes of service incidents while minimizing or preventing disruption to the customers. Problem management is the most proactive part of the resolution processes, although working very closely with the reactive part, incident management. It should proactively prevent the recurrence or replication of incidents or known errors.

Problem management is responsible for investigating and diagnosing the underlying causes of incidents. It ensures that up-to-date information on known errors and corrected problems is available to incident management.

Actions for improvement identified during this process should be recorded and input into the service improvement plan.

The problem management process includes:

- Initiation of problem management;

- Error control and resolution of problems;

- Communicating information;

- Tracking and escalation;

- Problem record closure;

- Problem reviews;

- Proactive problem prevention.

7.2.2   General

It is common, but not universal, for the problem management process to be managed alongside the incident management and service reporting process. If this is the case, staff who perform the processes have multiple roles, which should be identified. Alternatively, teams of staff with separate roles should work closely together following processes that are closely integrated.

The problem management process has both reactive and proactive aspects. Management of outstanding problems through to resolution within the agreed service level targets is the most reactive aspect of problem management. This is because the problem has already been identified and the problem management process is simply minimizing the business impact by ensuring timely resolution.

The proactive aspect is analysis of incidents in order to prevent recurrence, leading to improvements in the service. Service reports are fundamental to the proactive problem management process.

Problem management differs from incident management in that its main goal is the detection of underlying causes and their eradication or circumvention. In many situations this goal can be in direct conflict with the goals of incident management, which aims to restore the service to the customer as quickly as possible, at the risk of not eradicating the underlying cause. A good example of this conflict is a network that regularly fails; while it can be reset quickly, thus resolving the incident, the underlying problem may require more time to investigate and resolve, delaying the restoration of the service, costing more downtime but preventing recurrence.

It is important that procedures are in place to identify, minimize or avoid the impact of incidents and problems. The procedures should also define the recording, classification, updating, escalation, resolution and closure of all problems, with all problems being recorded. If this is not done the benefits of problem management are lost, even if incident management is done effectively.

Changes required in order to correct the underlying cause of problems should be passed to the change management process so that they are properly controlled and those involved are all working on the same basis.

Problem resolution itself should also be monitored, reviewed and reported on for effectiveness as part of this process.

Benefits

- Problems are prevented or, if they have occurred, recurrence is prevented.

- If problem resolution targets are at risk or not met, problems are escalated.

- Service levels are improved and costs reduced.

- Customer satisfaction is improved even if most customers are unaware of problem management as a process.

7.2.3 Initiation of problem management

Incidents should be classified in a way that assists problem management to identify the root cause of incidents. Incidents should reference existing problems and changes.

Prompt resolution of problems is assisted by reference to similar problems resolved previously. It is important to classify problems and record cross references to previously logged and resolved problems.

7.2.4   Error control and problem resolution

When the problem management investigation and diagnosis has identified the root cause of an incident and a method of resolving the incident, the problem should be classified and recorded as a known error.

All known errors should be recorded against the current and potentially affected services in addition to the configuration item suspected of being at fault.

Information on known errors in services being introduced into the live environment should be passed to service management and should be recorded in the knowledge base, together with any workarounds.

A known error should not be closed until after successful resolution.

The customer or supplier may decide that the resolution is too expensive or not of sufficient benefit to the business. If this is the case the circumstances and reasons for this decision should be clearly documented. The known error record should remain open however, since recurrence is likely, requiring workarounds and/or reassessment of the original decision on how to handle this specific known error.

When the root cause has been identified, and a decision to resolve it has been made, the resolution should be progressed via the change management process.

7.2.5   Communication of information

Information on workarounds, permanent fixes or progress of problems should be communicated to those affected or required to support affected services.

7.2.6   Tracking and escalation

The progress of all problems should be tracked. All issues should be escalated to the appropriate parties. The process should cover:

• Recording changes to the identities of those responsible for problem resolution during the lifecycle of each problem;

• Identification of incidents that breach service level targets;

• Cascading information to customers and colleagues so that they can take appropriate action to minimize the impact of the unresolved problem;

• Defining the escalation points;

• Recording of the resources used and any actions taken.

7.2.7   Incident and problem record closure

The record closure procedure should include checking to ensure that:

• Details of resolution have been accurately logged;

• The cause is categorized to facilitate analysis;

• If appropriate, both the customer and support staff are aware of the resolution;

• The customer agrees that the resolution has been achieved;

• If a resolution is not to be achieved or is not possible, the customer is informed.

7.2.8   Problem reviews

Problem reviews should be held when justified by investigation into unresolved, unusual or high-impact problems. Their purpose is to seek improvements to the process and to prevent recurrence of incidents or mistakes.

Problem reviews are typically:

• Reviews of individual incident levels and problem status against service levels;

• Management reviews to highlight those problems that require immediate action;

• Management reviews to determine and analyse trends and to provide input for other processes, e.g. customer education.

The reviews should include identification of:

• Trends (e.g. recurring problems and incidents, known errors, etc.);

• Recurring problems of a particular classification component or location;

• Deficiencies caused by resourcing, training or documentation;

• Non-conformances (e.g. against standards, policies and legislation);

• Known errors in planned releases;

• Staff resource commitment in resolving incidents and problems;

• Non-recurrence of resolved incidents or problems.

Improvements to the service or the problem management process should be recorded and fed into a service improvement plan for action. The information should be added to the problem management knowledge base.

All relevant documentation should be updated, e.g. user guides and system documentation.

7.2.9   Problem prevention

Proactive problem management should lead to a reduction in incidents and problems. It should include reference to information that assists analysis, e.g.:

- Asset and configuration;

- Change management;

- Published known error and workaround information from suppliers;

- Historical information on similar problems.

Problem prevention should range from prevention of individual incidents (e.g. repeated difficulties with a particular feature of a system) through to strategic decisions. The latter can require major expenditure to implement (e.g. investment in a better network): at this level proactive problem management merges into availability management.

Problem prevention also includes information being given to customers that means they do not need to ask for assistance in the future, e.g. preventing incidents caused by lack of user knowledge or training.

Possible problems

- If problem management is implemented either partly or badly the services are at risk. Partial implementation of problem management (e.g. monitoring outstanding calls but not analysing trends) means areas for improvement are not identified. This results in a lack of understanding of the root cause of any change to the level of services delivered, i.e. degraded service provision can often be understood by analysing the workload characteristics of problems.

- One of the most common reasons for failure of problem management is the absence of comprehensive detail on problems. This may be simply that only certain types of problem are logged or that those logging the problem do so without sufficient care and attention to detail. In either case the problem management process does not have reliable data to use for analysis and proactive problem prevention. This often occurs because those doing the logging do not understand (or perhaps care) how the information is to be used by anyone other than themselves.

8   Control processes

Configuration and change management enable an organization to control its assets and configurations and maintain configuration information. Accurate information enables better planning and control as changes are made and releases are distributed through the enterprise. Control processes and release processes apply to managing hardware and software assets, the infrastructure and configurations within the service. They support all the other service management processes by providing accurate information on the infrastructure and service configurations.

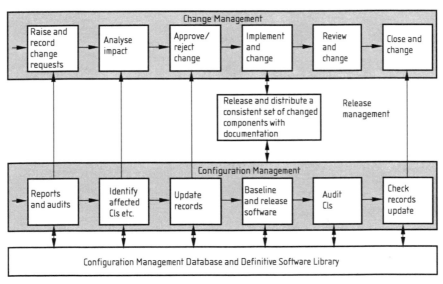

Figure 6: How the control processes work together

Configuration management involves the unique identification, recording and reporting of components, their versions, constituent components and relationships. Typical items include end-to-end service configurations, systems, products, hardware, system software, applications, commercial software and licences, documentation, people and facilities. In distributed environments, configuration items occur within many different configuration structures, e.g. a person may use a web browser that accesses a financial system on the other side of the world. A change to the web browser, network or system may affect this person and his/her business process.

The term "asset management" is largely synonymous with "configuration management", but is usually used for configuration items with a financial value. Asset management is the term used to describe the maintenance of details of hardware and software components, including licenses, and their location and interrelationships. It often includes the maintenance of financial details for each asset and interfaces to other processes, for example, procurement.

Uncontrolled change can lead to reduced service levels, lost customers, lost opportunities, lost money, fraud, fines, wasted resources, security breaches and can damage the organization's reputation or brand. Configuration management enables better control of changes. As businesses demand more change more quickly, service providers should be responsive while maintaining reliable, available and stable services. Change management ensures that the service provider works with the business to deliver changes that have maximum benefit while managing the impact and risk of change.

8.1 Configuration management

Objective

To define and control the components of the service and infrastructure and maintain accurate configuration information.

8.1.1 Scope of configuration management

Configuration management requires a policy on what should be controlled. Components with a unique identity that are to be controlled are referred to as configuration items. Typical configuration items are services, systems, products, hardware, system software, applications, commercial software and licences, documentation, people and facilities.

Configuration management should ensure that assets and configurations that fall within the scope of configuration management are identified, conform to their specifications and are documented in sufficient detail to support other processes. Configuration items should be managed through all stages of their lifetime through receipt, acceptance, installation, operation, maintenance, disposal and retirement. The scope of configuration management will influence other processes, e.g. the ability to diagnose in problem management and the ability to do impact analysis in change management.

Activities within configuration management include:

- Planning;

- Managing configuration data and information;

- Managing software, media and documentation;

- Identification;

- Configuration control;

- Configuration status accounting and reporting;

- Configuration audit and verification;

- Licence management.

8.1.2   General

Configuration management should be linked to change and release management to ensure that configuration information is updated as changes are made to the infrastructure and services. To achieve an adequate level of control the approach to configuration management should fit with the business drivers: the organization's and customer's requirements.

Planning should define the scope, objectives, policies, procedures, and the organizational and technical context for asset and configuration management. When managing configurations across distributed teams each part of the organization may develop a local plan within the context of an overall plan.

An organization's configuration management processes and data should be integrated with those of its customers and suppliers to ensure that accurate configuration management information accompanies the handover of any configurations, e.g. new releases and patches. This should include relevant tools, databases and processes where appropriate.

A good starting point is to identify and manage business critical services where there is ongoing change and a requirement for high availability and service continuity. This helps people to see the business benefits required to support further implementation. Implementing an appropriate level of automation will help to increase efficiency and reduce errors, e.g. automating the data collection and updating of configuration information will reduce errors and contribute to a good, economic solution.

Benefits

- A consistent, cost-effective and repeatable way of managing infrastructure and service configurations.

- Improved quality, stability and security of the infrastructure and services.

- Management and protection of assets.

- Contribution to compliance with legal, regulatory and contractual obligations.

- Better control of changes.

- Enables effective and efficient deployment and support of software and hardware.

- Provides good information on configurations that enables problems to be prevented or resolved more quickly.

- Provides valuable knowledge and configuration information to other processes, e.g. to improve resource planning and financial management.

- Fulfils legal obligations by controlling licences and preventing use of illegal copies of software.

- Improvement in speed and accuracy of configuration audits.

- Improved control, security and disaster recovery.

A good configuration management implementation should include the following actions:

- Identify and label all assets and configuration items with any necessary relationships;

- Support configuration items of varying complexity;

- Control all changes to configuration items;
- Establish and maintain baseline configurations;
- Provide accurate configuration information to other parties;
- Assist in identifying items that cause increases in incidents;
- Control valuable assets and help to identify costly unused equipment;
- Manage software licenses and identify costly unused licences;
- Protect the assets and intellectual capital of the organization;
- Ensure that only authorized copies of software are used;
- Conduct configuration audits to ensure that physical configurations match what is documented in the inventory;
- Train staff in the processes and tools;
- Provide reports to management on performance of the process.

8.1.3   Managing configuration data and information

Configuration information is maintained in an inventory, often called the configuration management database (CMDB). This logical database should provide information about the assets and configurations and information on software and document versions. It should provide information on what changes are planned, what items are undergoing change, what has been released, where assets are located, when warranty periods end and when licences should be renewed.

Many organizations have configuration data in simple lists or spreadsheets, often with gaps and inconsistencies in the data that should be resolved and managed. It is good practice to use a robust database. In large installations there may be several databases or data sources that comprise the logical CMDB. The data format and codes should be consistent across such databases. It is useful to use reporting tools to combine and present information from multiple configuration management sources.

Configuration management processes should ensure that information is updated when:

- New items are registered;
- Items are deleted/withdrawn or disposed/retired;
- The state of an item changes;
- Versions of configuration items are updated;

- Change requests and records are updated;

- Hardware, software or documentation are released, distributed or installed, particularly into acceptance test and production.

The resources required for configuration management often influence the policy on accuracy and level of detail of configuration management information. Achieving 100 % accurate data can be expensive without appropriate automation. However, if the information is frequently inaccurate staff and auditors will lose confidence in the data. If limited resources mean configuration management data is not accurate then it is advisable to reduce the scope and level of detail.

8.1.4   Managing software, media and documentation

Authorized versions of all software, media and documentation should be securely held in libraries and restricted to appropriate staff. The definitive software library (DSL) is a physical or electronic storage area where the authorized master versions and copies are stored.

8.1.5   Configuration identification

Configuration items (CIs) should be selected by decomposing (i.e. breaking down) the service and infrastructure according to agreed criteria, e.g. safety or mission critical, high risk, logistics, ease of maintenance. This should divide the total configuration structure into logically related and subordinate groups of hardware, software, services or combinations of these. Selecting too many CIs will affect visibility of the configurations, hamper management and increase costs. Selecting too few CIs with insufficient detail will create logistic and maintenance difficulties and limit control. The scope and degree of control should match the business needs.

Separating common components and interfaces helps to simplify the configuration structures and maintenance of the data.

Each item is assigned a unique identifier and linked to a manager who is responsible for ensuring that each configuration item and its configuration data is accurately maintained.

Configuration items should be defined by their functional and physical characteristics, e.g. description, type, purpose, version, size, location, components, relationships to other configuration items and current status.

Baselines list a consistent set of components with their version identifier. It is important to define when baselines should be established, e.g. after a set of specifications are signed off or before an application release into acceptance testing. Baselines form the basis for further activities, e.g. monitoring changes, verifying and auditing, and regression.

8.1.6 Configuration control

Configuration control ensures that only authorized and identifiable configuration items are accepted through to disposal. Items should be added, modified, replaced, or removed with appropriate controls, e.g. version control, approved change request, service request or other similar documentation. The processes should ensure that the inventory or CMDB is updated.

Access controls should provide staff with the correct level of access to the CMDB, physical hardware, software, media and documentation.

Build, release, distribution and installation controls should ensure that updated versions of software and hardware are built and distributed to target environments correctly.

The interface controls with suppliers and customers should cover the method of controlling configurations across organizations, e.g. delivering and installing software releases and patches.

8.1.7 Configuration status accounting and reporting

Status accounting should capture, correlate, store, maintain and provide views of the assets and configurations for different purposes, e.g. an application support team will want to see individual application modules when fixing software problems whereas, the Service Desk may only wish to track and report incidents and problems against the main application release.

Many incidents and problems are caused by people making changes without any knowledge of the full impact of the change or of other changes that are planned. It is therefore useful for staff to see what configuration is being planned or was planned, what is being changed or has been changed, and what was released. Typical reports are included in Annex B.

8.1.8 Configuration audit and verification

Audits and verification activities should be scheduled at appropriate intervals to ensure that:

* There is adequate control of the configurations (e.g. hardware,

software, media, licences and documentation);

- The physical configurations match the configuration information in the inventory/CMDB and related documentation;

- The actual function of a configuration item meets its specification.

Finding a discrepancy quickly saves time and effort, and reduces problems and embarrassment, e.g. verifying that planned configuration items are complete before release or on delivery from a supplier. The increase or decrease in discrepancies and nonconformities provide a measure of how well the control and release management processes are working.

Automation can significantly reduce the costs of auditing configurations, e.g. desktop configurations. Superfluous software, licences and equipment are often found during audits and their removal can reduce costs.

8.1.9 Licence management

In many countries companies and their directors are legally liable when software is used without legal title. Configuration and asset management should include managing and tracking the rights to use software, typically a license, from purchase to disposal. Responsibility for configuration and asset management, release management, finance, procurement and logistics should be clearly defined across functions.

Possible problems

- Immature culture and lack of understanding of what is involved.

- Lack of management commitment and support.

- The scope is too wide or the configurations are defined in too much detail for the resources available.

- Difficulty defining owners of configuration items and their configuration data.

- Inadequate or untested release, distribution and installation processes.

- Configuration management is perceived to be too bureaucratic, giving excuses to circumvent the process.

- Achieving an integrated solution across the life cycle and with other organizations can be difficult and expensive.

- Over reliance on manual processes that are resource intensive, causing staff to become overloaded and the processes inefficient and error prone.

- Lack of adequate tools to support the integrated processes economically.

8.2 Change management

Objective

To ensure all changes are assessed, approved, implemented and reviewed in a controlled manner.

8.2.1 Scope

Change management helps organizations to maximize the benefits of making changes while minimizing disruption to service. Poorly managed changes result in an increase in incidents and problems and service levels can degrade rapidly. Unsuccessful changes also waste valuable effort on unplanned activities that result in chaos while everyone tries to recover.

Change management works closely with configuration management to ensure that all changes to components are properly documented in the inventory or CMDB. This ensures that when a change is made the correct versions and releases are released into the right environment. Change and configuration management should be planned together.

Changes to services or the infrastructure can arise in response to problems or externally imposed requirements, e.g. business, commercial, technology, policy or legislative changes; service improvements and supplier changes. Configuration management defines the scope and depth of configuration items to be formally controlled by change management.

Change management includes the overall approach for:

- Grouping changes;

- Determining the type of change workflow or model to follow;

- Classification, prioritization and impact analyses;
- Authorization of different types of change.

The activities for managing individual changes are:

- Raising, recording and classifying changes;
- Assessing the impact, urgency, cost, benefits and risk of change;
- Obtaining approval;
- Implementing the change;
- Testing, verifying and signing off;
- Closing and reviewing the change.

8.2.2 General

For greater efficiency, different types of proposed change can have different workflows, e.g. a "normal" request for change may have a longer workflow than a routine or standard change. It is good practice to ensure that the workflow states are consistent across the organization so that there are no misunderstandings, particularly in global implementations.

Emergency or urgent changes are sometimes required and where possible should follow the change workflow, but some details may be documented retrospectively. The change should be reviewed afterwards to verify that it was a true emergency.

The levels of authorization for a particular type of change should be judged by the size or risk of the change, e.g. changes in a large enterprise that affect several distributed sites may need to be approved by a higher- level change authority such as a global change board or the Board of Directors.

When a request for change (RFC) is raised it is important that good quality information is recorded against a clearly defined service or configuration item to ensure that the whole process works efficiently.

An RFC should record information such as: a unique reference, the name of the person raising the change, a description and identification of affected configuration items and versions, the reason and resources to analyse or implement the change. It should also include the justification and business benefits.

The RFC should include:

- Classification of the type of change (e.g. urgent/emergency, high, normal, low);

- The category of change (e.g. major, minor impact);

- Reference to any documents associated with the originating of the change (e.g. problems and known errors, purchase orders, other RFC).

Benefits

- Better alignment of services to actual business needs by making changes more quickly and successfully.

- Changes that maximize business benefit are approved and implemented.

- Better impact and risk management of changes reduces the number of failed changes or changes that have to be backed out.

- Improved visibility of changes across distributed enterprises.

- Reduction in uncontrolled change that causes disruption to users and the business.

- Changes are controlled and can be backed out to a previous state.

8.2.3 Assessing the impact and risk of changes

Since most services and systems are heavily interrelated, any change made in one part of a service or the infrastructure can have profound impacts on another part.

Configuration management provides configuration information to assist with impact analysis.

Change management should identify all affected parties and components in order to mitigate or eliminate any adverse effects. Each affected party should assess the risk, impact and business benefit of each change.

Change management ensures there is a valid business justification for making the change and summarizes the impacts in preparation for approval.

8.2.4 Change approval and change advisory boards

The change authority or board should consider requests for change and make recommendations on whether a change should be accepted or rejected. The change authority can be a person (e.g. the Change Manager), or a group (e.g. a Change Advisory Board, CAB).

Meetings and decisions can be held using electronic communications, however, physical meetings are very useful during periods of major change or when there are high volumes of incidents, often caused by change.

An agenda should be circulated for meetings and decisions documented.

8.2.5   Scheduling and implementing a change

The status of changes and scheduled implementation dates should be used as the basis for change and release scheduling.

A forward schedule of changes should be maintained and communicated to the groups and people affected by the changes. Where an outage may be caused during normal service hours the people affected should agree to the change before implementation.

Approved RFCs should be passed to the applicable groups responsible for procurement, development or implementation of new, changed or disposed components. The configuration information should be updated at each step to ensure that the inventory or CMDB remains accurate and that staff can see the status of configuration items undergoing change. Change management should be notified of implemented changes.

8.2.6   Closing and reviewing the change request

A change should be closed if there are no unexpected side-effects and when the originator, customer or user representative agrees that the change is complete. All documentation, including the CMDB, should be properly updated to reflect the change, e.g. actual resources used and costs incurred.

All changes should be reviewed for success or failure after implementation and any actions recorded. For significant changes a post-implementation review should be held to check that the change met its objectives, that customers are happy with the results and that there have been no unexpected side-effects.

Lessons learned should be fed back into future changes or into service improvement.

8.2.7 Change management analysis and reporting

Useful management information can be produced from change management, e.g. regular reports on the status of changes. Reports should be available to all relevant parties. It is extremely useful for the service desk to know what changes happened in the last week and what changes are planned in the coming weeks.

Change records should be analysed regularly to detect increasing levels of changes, frequently recurring types, emerging trends and other relevant information. Typical reports are listed in Annex B.

Possible problems

- The scope of a change is too wide for the resources available, overstretching the staff and causing delays.

- Lack of knowledge of the impact of proposed changes and inaccurate configuration information can result in delays and incomplete assessments.

- The process is too bureaucratic, giving excuses for not following it.

- Too many dependencies and poor synchronization of upgrades between platforms and across locations make changes difficult to schedule.

- Back-out procedures are missing or untested.

- Progressing change requests is manually intensive (it is advisable to start with a simple database or an automated system).

- Lack of backing from senior and middle managers lengthens implementation times and staff resist the controls that they would prefer to avoid.

- The process frequently fails when emergency changes are to be done.

9 Release processes

9.1 Release management

Objective

To deliver, distribute and track one or more changes in a release into the live environment.

9.1.1 Scope

Release management includes the following to create a defined set of release components:

- Setting the release policy;

- Release and roll-out planning;

- Developing or acquiring software;

- Designing, building and configuring release;

- Release verification and acceptance;

- Roll-out, distribution and installation.

Release management uses:

- Information from the CMDB;

- The definitive software library (DSL) that contains all master copies of controlled software and electronic assets;

- The definitive hardware store (DHS) that contains spares and stocks of hardware.

The release processes work closely with the change and configuration management to ensure that the shared CMDB is up to date. A release should be under change management and the content and timing of a release should be authorized in advance via change management.

9.1.2 General

A release is a set of authorized changes that consist of new or changed configuration items. The changes are planned, tested and implemented into the live environment together. Several service providers and suppliers may be involved in a release in a distributed environment, e.g. client server and e-commerce applications. Release management coordinates the activities of the service provider, many suppliers and the business, to plan and deliver a release successfully while protecting the quality of the live environment.

The approach to releasing a set of website updates can be much simpler than a complex software release. The type of release and related release procedures should reflect this. To reduce disruption to the live environment it is often better to minimize the number of releases, particularly where complex software changes are involved. Many changes can be grouped into one release if the business and its customers can handle the amount of change involved.

The main advantage of packaging many changes into a release is that all components are built, tested, distributed and implemented together. However, the additional effort and resources required for a full release may be too great and a partial release may be more effective, e.g. a low risk standard update to virus protection software could be a partial release.

The main roles and responsibilities in release management should be defined in a release policy to ensure that everyone understands their role and level of authority. The release policy should include:

- The frequency and type of release with expected deliverables;
- The business critical times that mean the risk of a change is high;
- The unique identification and description of the release units;
- The approach to grouping changes into a release;
- The approach to automating the build, installation, release and distribution of changes;
- The verification and acceptance of a release.

The costs associated with setting up release management can include:

- Dedicated staff to plan and manage the implementation of a release across the distributed groups;

- CMDB, systems and tools;
- Distribution and installation software tools and environments.

Benefits

- Minimizes disruption and risk to the business due to poorly planned software releases.
- Reduces incidents and improves quality of services as software and hardware are tested together in an environment that is similar to live.
- Provides a repeatable process for rolling out new software and hardware with related business changes.
- Enables a release to be rolled out quickly and cost-effectively.
- Sets customer and staff expectations.
- Releases are well planned and resources are scheduled in advance.
- Release documentation enables problem, change and configuration management records to be updated efficiently and in a timely manner.

9.1.3 Release and roll-out planning

Good planning and management are essential to package and successfully distribute a release, and to manage the associated impacts and risks to the business and IT. Plans should be prepared, agreed and communicated to all relevant business and support groups. The service provider should work proactively with the business and its suppliers to ensure that the configuration items in the release are compatible.

The roll-out may be planned in stages, as details of the roll-out may not be known initially. Plans on how to roll out the release should detail exactly how, when and who will do what during the last implementation steps.

Information for planning should be based on the master information in the CMDB. Audits of the production environment (e.g. servers and PCs) may also be required for major upgrades to ensure that there are no surprises during the roll-out. The plan should define the logistics and processes to purchase, store, dispatch, accept and dispose of goods. Extra support resources should be planned during major upgrades to ensure that the service levels are maintained.

The release may be phased (e.g. by geographical location) and the release plan should contain dates for each location, training session and installation. The plans should include how to manage and track the tasks that are to be undertaken by support groups and individuals across the enterprise. These should be reviewed and signed off by all parties involved.

9.1.4 Design, build and configure release

Release and distribution mechanisms should be designed and implemented to comply with the organization's architecture, standards and business processes (e.g. procurement and logistics). It is important to ensure that the integrity of the release is maintained during build, installation, handling, packaging and delivery. It is best practice to check that the target platform satisfies prerequisites before installation. Automating the build, installation, release and distribution processes reduces errors and ensures that the process is repeatable, which helps to roll out new releases quickly. The configuration management database should provide this information.

All master copies of the software or electronic files to be used in the build or release should be taken from controlled libraries, e.g. Definitive Software Library (DSL). The software licence holding and software licence information should be updated during the release process. Automating the build, installation, release and distribution processes should reduce errors and ensure that the process is repeatable, efficient and successful.

Output deliverables from the build activity, e.g. delivery note, release note, installation instructions, installed software and hardware with related configuration information, should be handed over to the group responsible for testing. The build inputs and outputs are placed under configuration management and stored in DSL to enable recovery from disaster or failed changes.

9.1.5 Release verification and acceptance

The business, customer and service provider staff should be prepared and ready to accept the release into the live environment. It helps if key staff and users are involved in the requirements and acceptance phases. An appropriate release authority should sign off each stage of acceptance testing. The end result should be a sign-off on completeness of the whole release package against the requirements. The verification and acceptance processes should ensure that an appropriate level of testing has been completed (e.g. functional and non-functional testing, business acceptance testing and testing of the build, release, distribution and installation procedures).

The logistics, distribution and installation mechanisms should verify that a release is complete when it reaches its destination and that any configuration information has been updated. Appropriate documentation should be available on completion and stored under configuration management against the released configuration item (e.g. release documents, service documents, support procedures and licences). Incident management should be informed of known errors. If the release is rejected, delayed or cancelled, change management should be informed.

9.1.6   Roll-out, distribution and installation

The roll-out processes should ensure that equipment and software are delivered safely to their destination. This usually includes many other processes and functions within the organization (e.g. change and configuration management, logistics, health, safety and electrical checks). It is essential to ensure that secure storage areas are provided for software and hardware. Redundant products, services and licences should be decommissioned as part of the roll-out activity.

End customers often perform a final acceptance test of the installed software, e.g. a desktop upgrade. For substantial changes the customers should develop or be given a checklist of tests to perform. An installation satisfaction survey is useful to provide feedback. After a successful installation, the configuration information should be updated with the location and the owner of the hardware and software. This will assist support staff to locate equipment and resolve incidents and problems more efficiently.

The number of incidents related to the release in the period immediately following a roll-out should be measured and analysed to assess their impact on the business, operations and support staff resources. The change management process should include a post-implementation review for the whole release.

Possible problems

- A lack of understanding of who is responsible for managing components of the release at different points of the release cycle and environments.

- Insufficient resources available to provide for adequate acceptance testing.

- Insufficient staff, machine and network resources to build and test new releases and equipment adequately.

- Testing in one area being acceptable but failing in another area, e.g. different infrastructure, or parameters not set the same.

- A lack of understanding of the release contents, build and installation components, and their inter-dependencies, leading to mistakes.

- Insufficient local control of desktop computers, servers and networks at distributed sites.

- Making too many assumptions when planning the roll-out across different cultural and geographical groups.

- Staff reluctant to back out a release and there is pressure to transfer inadequately.

10 Automation of service management

10.1 Scope

Implementing tools allows an organization to automate the service management processes and centralize key functions. The range and sophistication of tools for service management automation has grown rapidly in recent years. Tools should be used to complement and enhance service delivery, not replace it.

Typical types of service management solutions to support the core processes are:

- Service desk or help desk, with or without a CMDB;

- Integrated service management tools comprising modern client-server-based tools, with or without a knowledge database.

Automation options include:

- Technology such as computer telephone integration (CTI) or voice over internet protocol (VOIP);

- Interactive voice response systems (IVR);

- The Internet, e-mail, voice mail, fax;

- Calls to pagers, mobiles, laptops, personal digital assistants;

- Self-help knowledge bases;

- Case based reasoning/search systems;

- Remote diagnostic tools;

- Workflow capability to manage and track progress;

- Automated system and network management tools;

- Intranet and self service platforms;

- Remote release and distribution;

- Configuration discovery, collection and audit tools;
- Security monitoring and control, including password control, detection of violations and virus protection;
- Performance and capacity planning;
- Contingency management (including automatic backups);
- Reporting and visualization tools that access several databases.

The Internet and intranets provide useful facilities for service management in global, local and distributed environments. These include:

- General marketing;
- E-mail;
- Supplier program fixes and upgrades;
- Publishing of known errors;
- Customer notice boards;
- Knowledge searches;
- A common cross platform user interface;
- Software fixes which can be downloaded either by support staff or customers themselves;
- Solutions to known problems, which can be searched for to reduce problem solving time.

10.2 General

Tools such as call logging and problem tracking have been supplemented by remote support capabilities and software capable of handling complex and multiple SLAs (with separate targets and business clocks).

Many service management tools interface with the Internet (usually as an intranet), enabling access to tools in a distributed environment.

Many enterprises have introduced staff regulations restricting the use of the Internet and downloading software from it. This is prudent as it protects the customers as a whole, but can be very unpopular. It may be resisted and can be difficult to police.

Automation that provides support for distributed computing has revolutionized the ability of an enterprise to diagnose problems remotely, and in many cases also to fix them remotely and therefore more quickly. Remote support technology has also made it possible for an enterprise to make changes by downloading the new versions of software and to monitor the capacity of the infrastructure, identifying capacity problems before they become serious.

> ## Benefits
>
> - Reduces costs by reducing repetitive manual tasks, e.g. workload monitoring and service reporting.
>
> - Improves the cost-effectiveness and speed of service management processes.
>
> - Provides cost-effective control of the services.
>
> - Enables the centralization of key functions with fewer administrators.
>
> - Improves the analysis of raw data and the identification of trends.
>
> - Enables the implementation of preventive measures.

10.3 Selecting and implementing automated solutions

Each tool for the automation of service management has advantages and disadvantages. In a very small organization a simple database system may be sufficient for logging and controlling incidents. However, in a very large organization, a sophisticated distributed integrated service management toolset may be required, linking all processes with event-management systems.

Workflow management provides a communications backbone for service management in large service organizations (e.g. to link each task in the life cycle from a new service being planned through to disposal). However, after a merger or major reorganization the workflow states may need to be re-engineered to support other groups with existing data.

The following should be considered when selecting tools:

- The fit with the organization's technical platforms and architectures;

- Existing tools that should be interfaced;

- A sound data structure;

- The integration capabilities;

- The ease of use;

- Support for multiple languages;

- Management information and performance reporting;

- Visualization (e.g. of network configuration managements);

- The ability to interface other tools (e.g. reporting and visualization tools);

- The process capability (e.g. support for best practices described by ITIL);

- The ability to load information automatically (e.g. from audit tools);

- An 80 % fit to operational requirements;

- The meeting of all mandatory requirements;

- Little (if any) product customization;

- The administration and maintenance costs within budget;

- The current user base and feedback from reference sites;

- The ability of the supplier to provide support;

- The costs of the product, training, consultancy and maintenance.

With service management tools it is important to ensure that the combination of technology, processes and people are integrated and meet the needs of the customers. Automation should be used to enhance service management, not replace it. To select and implement automated solutions it is good practice to use a project management method as this ensures the technology, data, people and process changes are implemented together.

10.4 Major change programmes

Many tools can help with major change programmes (e.g. asset, configuration, change and release management and capacity planning). If tools are well established with good procedures for their use, they can be assessed for use in major programmes of change.

10.5 Practical success factors for automation

The cost of purchasing tools will be much less than the total cost of implementation. As well as tools the following should be budgeted for:

- Hardware, accommodation and consumables;
- Time for preparing for implementation, data gathering and conversion, and testing;
- Management time for decisions required throughout the project;
- Training of staff to use, administer and support the tools and related processes.

To successfully automate service management and implement tools it is important to:

- Use a good project management method;
- Define the objectives and requirements for automation;
- Get buy-in from the relevant stakeholders and staff;
- Have formal selection criteria;
- Consider parallel running of old and new tools;
- Phase the implementation with feedback sought at each stage;
- Accommodate integration with other tools and databases;
- Ensure look-up lists are short, meaningful and concise;
- Look for simple tools or process improvements for gaps discovered during development and implementation.

Possible problems

- Unrealistic expectations of the tool mean there is rapid loss of enthusiasm.
- Workflow set-up is perceived to be too bureaucratic and the tool is blamed.
- Sophisticated tools introduced into organizations with an immature culture.
- Inadequate resources for the implementation, particularly staff implementing tools while also doing their operational jobs.
- Implementation of tools that do not adequately support process integration.

- Tools selected impose an unsuitable process.

- It may not be possible (or cost-effective) to convert data for a replacement tool.

- A faulty process remains faulty when automated.

- Failure to train staff adequately in the use of the tools.

Annex A: Guidance on SLAs

A.1 Defining the SLA structure

It is important that the structure of the master and the individual SLAs is agreed with customers early in their development (e.g. should there be one or many SLAs? what level of detail is required by the customers? and what service targets are the most appropriate representation of the customer's business requirements?).

The SLA structure should be manageable for the SLM function and should meet customer's business requirements, taking into account:

- Geographical placement;
- Organizational structure and management hierarchy;
- Number and types of business groups;
- Differences in services required inter and intra-business groups;
- Frequency of changes to the SLA.

The structure should be agreed by the supplier and customer management.

A.2 Contents of a sample SLA

It is usually preferable to include references to other documents in each SLA rather than include detail common to several SLAs, e.g. procedures common to several services. It is counter-productive to include a large number of targets or workload measures. A large number of targets can distract attention from those that describe business critical components of the service.

The cost of monitoring and reporting on a wide range of service issues can outweigh the benefits and will be seen as an unacceptable overhead. A master SLA can be used for this purpose. The non-prescriptive list is included to prompt the development of an SLA which is appropriate to the service(s) in question. This list should not be used in its entirety as the basis for an SLA. The SLA can include some of the following information according to the service in question:

- Brief service and business critical issues description;
- Validity period and/or SLA change control mechanism;
- Authorization details;
- Brief description of communications, including:
  - contact points;
  - communications channels/methods;
  - reports and service reviews/references (to other processes).
- Names and means of contacting people authorized to act in emergencies by participating in problem correction, recovery or workaround;
- Service hours, e.g.:
  - 9:00 to 17:00;
  - date exceptions (e.g. weekends, public holidays);
  - critical business periods.
- Scheduled and agreed interruptions, including:
  - type and notice to be given;
  - number per period.
- Customer responsibilities such as:
  - delivery of input media;
  - response to instructions to log off at end of day;
  - protection of security identities;
  - control of the media on the desktop.
- Service provider liability and obligations, e.g.:
  - security;
  - impact and priority guidelines;
  - escalation and notification process;
  - complaints procedure.

- Service targets, e.g.:
  - system response times;
  - reliability/availability (is it available when it is needed?).
- Workload limits (upper and lower), e.g. the ability of the service to support the agreed number of customers/volume of work, system throughput.
- High-level financial management details, e.g. charge codes, etc.
- Action to be taken in the event of a service interruption;
- Housekeeping/data security, including how this is achieved and how the service is affected by it;
- Glossary of terms;
- Supporting and related services;
- Any exceptions;
- Statement of the supplier's obligations regarding such matters as:
  - report production schedule;
  - on-line availability and performance;
  - fault response;
  - recovery times for various types of failure.
- Functionality (i.e. does the system do all the right things correctly);
- Disaster recovery;
- Charging/budget details.

A.3   Guidelines for service level targets

The guidance given below does not preclude the use of different measures within an individual SLA, if appropriate.

Targets to consider were highlighted in the description of the SLA structure. Any of the measures listed as reports in Annex B could be used as a target in an SLA. Targets should not be included in the SLA unless they can be monitored and reported with adequate accuracy but without excessive costs being incurred. Choice of targets should also take into account which aspects of the service matter most to the customers.

The same reasoning applies to SLAs, OLAs and third-party contracts. The following should be determined:

- Whether the targets and workload measurements are concise, relevant to customer needs and measurable;

- Whether any targets are potentially ambiguous (e.g. is the method of calculating availability understood by both supplier and customers?);

- Whether any of the targets are duplicates because they cover the same or similar aspects of the service;

- Whether the targets and workload measurements incorporated into the individual SLAs will be easily understood so that they can be used as part of the SLM process.

Annex B: Service management reports

B.1   Workload and problem management reports

It is neither useful nor cost-effective to report a very large number of metrics, even if a large number is monitored and could be reported regularly. Complex reports can confuse or mislead the reader. The reports produced by the problem management activity provide valuable input to the service management function. The following list, although not exhaustive, gives information that may be incorporated into service management reports.

- Telephone calls:
    - number and percentage of inbound and outbound;
    - number of calls per support person receiving calls, also as a percentage of all calls, per support person;
    - queue times;
    - number and percentage of abandoned;
    - number and percentage of to voice mail;
    - number and percentage of picked up in x seconds;
    - wait time to call pick up;
    - staff performance;
    - staff availability to take telephone calls;
    - duration;
    - profile throughout day, week, month, year;
    - out of hours.
- Number and percentage of calls/requests logged of types:
    - incident/problems;

- service requests;

- changes.

- Number and percentage of calls/requests logged in each status e.g. logged, resolved, closed.

- Number and percentage of resolved calls/requests and (separately) outstanding calls/requests, by:

  - location/time zone;

  - business area;

  - type;

  - severity and priority;

  - service provider (including third-party suppliers);

  - problem solver;

  - overall.

- Number and percentage of calls/requests resolved on the telephone or by prompt return communication:

  - overall;

  - by service provider;

  - by problem solver.

- Number and percentage of calls/requests not acted upon within agreed service levels, broken down by:

  - call type (especially the most common types);

  - resolving group;

  - customer business area;

  - severity.

- Number and percentage of calls/requests received per period and per customer business area by:

  - category;

  - severity;

  - CI.

- Number, percentage and types of escalated calls/requests;

- Type of requests consuming the most staff/third-party resource;

- Type of requests taking the longest time to turn around to customers;

- Customers, applications and equipment requiring the most support;

- Type of requests causing the highest business impact and associated costs;

- Customer satisfaction and perception;

- Identified training needs for:

  - customers;

  - support groups;

  - individual staff;

  - configuration item (e.g. specific application, type of hardware).

B.2   Financial reports

Financial reports should include:

- Total costs and total charges against budget comparisons;

- Values of assets and the cost of depreciation;

- Cost per service unit, with units such as:

  - per problem;

  - per customer,

  - per item of hardware, e.g. a PC;

  - per unit of storage.

B.3   Asset and configuration management reports

Asset management reports should include:

- Number of assets by type (including software licenses);

- Value of assets;

- Location of assets and assets by business units.

Configuration management reports should include:

- Selected configuration items, their components, version and status, associated documentation, dependencies and related changes and problems, to provide an overall view of the quality level of the configuration items;

- All the components in a service system: change, baseline, build or release, version or variant, e.g. build or baseline list;
- Current and historical data for each configuration item as it has progressed through its lifecycle, e.g. through ordered, received, in acceptance test, live, under change, withdrawn, disposed.

Configuration items that change frequently require high levels of support or cause many incidents and outages for the business.

A report for a CI may include the unique label, description, current status, owner responsible for change, change history, open problems/requests for change.

B.4   Change management reports

Change management reports can include all or some of the following:

- Number of change requests;
- Number and percentage of changes which were:
  - rejected;
  - emergencies;
  - in change status.
- Number and percentage of changes awaiting implementation by:
  - category;
  - time outstanding.
- Number and percentage of implemented changes by:
  - configuration component;
  - service.
- Change backlogs and bottlenecks;
- Costs per change and cost summaries;
- Business impact of changes;
- Changes by business area;
- Frequency of change to CIs;
- Status reports support service management activities, e.g. progress monitoring, problem management, change control, release management, configuration audits and service planning;

- Information should also be available on the validity period of contracts, SLAs or SLOs, and the value of any services, including those provided by third-party suppliers.

Annex C: Preparing for a BS 15000 audit

C.1   Scoping the managed service

When seeking certification a service provider should state the scope of the service to be audited and agree this with the auditor in advance of the audit. The scope statement should be confirmed by the auditor, referenced in the audit report and stated on any certificate of conformity. The scope statement should cover:

- The basis on which audits are conducted and certification is granted;

- The boundary of its service and service management activities, e.g.:

  - geographic boundaries;

  - organizational boundaries;

- Those processes that require full assessment or audit and those which require the interfaces to be considered.

C.2   Care in defining and maintaining the scope statement

Those who wish to take assurance from a service provider's certificate ought to ask to see the scope statement. It is therefore important that this is unambiguous and accurate. The audit certificate should not intentionally or unintentionally imply that the certified service provider has capabilities over and above those covered by the assessment. The auditor should ensure that the declared scope accurately describes the actual scope of the assessment.

If at any time during a service provider's certification cycle (e.g. during repeat audit checks) the auditor determines that the declared scope has changed, then the certificate, and possibly the basis of the certificate, will need to be amended.

The terms of a service contract cannot remove or reduce the obligation on the auditor to obtain sufficient appropriate evidence of conformity to the specified requirements. It might therefore be necessary to perform audit procedures within another organization in order to obtain that evidence.

In common with other standards, a BS 15000 certificate can be awarded only to an organization that is a single legal entity or part of a legal entity.

A single certificate cannot be awarded to organizations that are formed from more than one legal entity, even if the service management processes cross the boundaries between them. This restriction applies whatever the basis of ownership of the organisations

The certificate may be awarded to an organizational unit that forms part of a legal entity. That this is part of an organisation will be defined in the scope statement.

C.3   Seeking certification

By definition, the service provider is the organization that seeks certification. The term service provider is used with this meaning throughout this section.

The service provider should demonstrate their control over the relevant services delivered by suppliers, via service management processes, and that service levels and any other measures of service quality are monitored and reported objectively and meet the agreed needs of the customer.

It will generally be appropriate for certification to be awarded only to the service provider of the majority of the service/service management processes in the scope of the audit. BS 15000 is intended for service providers of all service management processes and is not appropriate for service providers who do only some of the processes.

For certification, it is unimportant whether processes within the scope of the audit are performed entirely by a single organizational unit, as the requirements of BS 15000 are independent of organizational form. However, if relevant processes are performed by units that are not part of the service provider's organization, certification might rely on a contribution by another organization. The other organisation may be another (third-party) supplier or it may be a customer.

C.4   What happens when more than one organization is involved?

It is not necessary for all organizations in a supply chain to achieve

BS 15000 for the service provider to gain certification, as long as the service provider can demonstrate that they control their suppliers, manage the interfaces effectively and control the data that flows either way across the interfaces. However, where multiple organizations are involved, the following apply:

- A service provider aspiring to certification is required to comply with the requirements for each process within the scope of BS 15000, or, where the service provider seeking certification does not have direct responsibility for every process in BS 15000, it should be possible to demonstrate that another organization has auditable service management processes of the correct standard, with interfaces controlled by the service provider.

- If certification is sought by a service provider reliant on third-party suppliers contributing to the attainment, the third-party suppliers would not as a consequence of the contribution gain certification through this mechanism. The third-party suppliers would have to be audited and found to be meeting the required standard for the service provider seeking certification to be successful. Only those processes that directly contribute to the service provider's certification should be audited.

- Where a service provider seeking certification has a contract to supply services, i.e. it is itself a third-party supplier to a customer who is also a supplier, it may still attain certification if the customer for those services contributes to the attainment. Gaining a certificate as a service provider in these circumstances is possible only if the contribution by the customer to the certification is included in the audit. The customer would not as a consequence of their contribution gain a certificate through this mechanism.

- Where there are multiple suppliers and customers involved in an audit it is essential that the scope of the service be defined as only the service sustained by the service management processes audited. At one extreme, the whole service may be the scope of the certificate. However, in many cases the scope will be limited to a specific service provided by the service provider to a specific customer or a range of services to several customers, including their own "in-house" colleagues. It will not be possible for a service provider to attain certification for all services or all customers on the basis of achieving the required standard for a service to just one of the customers.

- Where a service provider seeking certification provides the service to multiple customers or multiple locations, the auditor(s) will be expected to use their judgement on the number of customers or locations that should be audited, based on an understanding of the complexity of the arrangement and the variety of services offered.

- For the purposes of certification it is irrelevant which of the parties is defined in a contract (or SLA) as the supplier and which is defined as the customer. However, as the intent of BS 15000 is that certification is possible for service providers who have adopted best practices for *all* the processes specified in BS 15000, the auditor(s) will be expected to use their judgement on the validity of an attempt to gain certification if it is sought by a service provider that provides only some of the service/service management processes. It will generally be appropriate for certification to be awarded only to a service provider that is the supplier of the majority of the service/service management processes.

- It is particularly important to make the scope unambiguous where multiple organizations contribute to the service management processes being audited.

Annex D: Bibliography and other sources of information

D.1 Standards

The following referenced documents are indispensable for a more detailed understanding of this guide.

BS 7799-2:2002, *Information security management systems — Specification with guidance for use.*

BS 8600:1999, *Complaints management systems — Guide to design and implementation.*

BS 15000-1:2002, *IT service management — Part 1: Specification for service management.*

BS 15000-2:2002, *IT service management — Part 2: Code of practice for service management.*

BS EN ISO 9000:2000, *Quality management systems — Fundamentals and vocabulary.*

BS EN ISO 9001:2000, *Quality management systems — Requirements.*

BS EN ISO 9004:2000, *Quality management systems — Guidelines for performance improvement.*

BS EN ISO 10007:1997, *Quality management. Guidelines for configuration management.*

BS EN ISO 19011:2002, *Guidelines for quality and/or environmental management systems auditing.*

BS ISO/IEC 17799:2000 (BS 7799-1:2000), *Information technology — Code of practice for information security management.*

D.2 Other publications from standards bodies

Code of practice for legal admissibility and evidential weight of information stored electronically (ref: BIP 0008).

The principles of good practice for information management.
(ref: PD 0010)

IT Service Management — Self-assessment Workbook (ref: PD 0015)

Guide to BS 7799 risk assessment (ref: PD 3002)

D.3   Other publications

GREAT BRITAIN. Data Protection Act 1998. London: The Stationery Office.[2]

GREAT BRITAIN. Computer Misuse Act 1990. London: The Stationery Office.[2]

GREAT BRITAIN. Copyright, Designs and Patent Act 1988. London: The Stationery Office.[2]

ITIL Best Practice for Service Support. ISBN 0113300158.[2]

ITIL Best Practice for Service Delivery. ISBN 0113300174.[2]

ITIL Best Practice for Software Asset Management. ISBN 011330943.[2]

The IT Service Management Forum (itSMF), *Pocket Guide to IT Service Management*. ISBN 0952470616.[2]

The IT Service Management Forum (itSMF), *Dictionary of IT Service Management: Terms, Abbreviations and Acronyms*. ISBN 0952470659.[2]

TickIT Guide, *Using ISO 9001:2000 for Software Quality Management System Construction, Certification and Continual Improvement*, Issue 5.0. ISBN 0580369439.[2][3]

BuyIT Guidelines, Best practice notes to improve the way organisations specify, acquire and benefit from information systems.
ISBN 1900945002.[2]

D.4   Organizations

British Computer Society (BCS), 1 Stanford Street, Swindon, SN1 1HJ, UK.
Tel: +44(0)1793 417433, Fax: +44(0)1793 480270,
e-mail: bcshq@hq.bcs.org.uk, website: http://www.bcs.org.uk.

[2] Available from The Stationery Office, 51 Nine Elms Lane, London, SW8 5DR Tel: +44(0)870 600 5522, Fax +44(0)870 600 5533, e-mail: customer.services@tso.co.uk, website: http//www.tso.co.uk.

[3] For further information contact the TickIT Office, British Standards Institution, 389 Chiswick High Road, London W4 4AL. Tel +44(0) 20 8996 7427, Fax +44(0) 20 8996 7429, website:http://www.tickit.org.

British Computer Society Configuration Management Specialist Group.
e-mail: chair@bcs-cmsg.org.uk, website: http://www.bcs-cmsg.org.uk.

The Chartered Institute of Purchasing and Supply (CIPS), Easton House,
Easton on the Hill, Stamford, Lincolnshire, PE9 3NZ, UK.
Tel: +44(0)1780 756777, Fax: +44(0)1780 751610,
website: http://www.cips.org.

IT Service Management Forum (itSMF), Webbs Court, 8 Holmes Road,
Earley, Reading, RG6 7BH, UK. Tel: +44(0)118 926 0888,
Fax: +44(0)118 926 3073, e-mail: service@itsmf.com,
website: http://www.itsmf.com.

EXIN, Kantoor Janssoenborch, Hoog Catharijne, Godebaldkwartier 365,
3511 DT Utrecht, Postbus 19147, 3501 DC Utrecht, Netherlands.
Tel: (030) 234 4811, Fax: (030) 231 5986, e-mail: info@exin.nl,
website: http://www.exin.nl.

Federation Against Software Theft (FAST), Clivemont House,
54 Clivemont Road, Maidenhead, Berkshire, SL6 7BZ, UK.
Tel: +44(0)1628 622 121, Fax: +44(0)1628 760 355, e-mail: fast@fast.org,
website: http://www.fast.org.uk.

Information Systems Examination Board (ISEB), The British Computer
Society, 1 Sanford Street, Swindon, Wiltshire, SN1 1HJ, UK.
Tel: +44(0)1793 417 542, Fax: +44(0)1793 480 270,
e-mail: isebenq@hq.bcs.org.uk, website: http://www.bcs.org.uk/iseb.

Office of Government Commerce (OGC), Rosebery Court,
St Andrew's Business Park, Norwich, Norfolk, NR7 OHS, UK.
Tel: +44(0)845 000 4999, e-mail: ServiceDesk@ogc.gsi.gov.uk,
website: http://www.ogc.gov.uk.

D.5 Maturity models and maturity measurements

COBIT, Control Objectives for IT and related Technology from the IT
Governance Institute and the Information Systems Audit and Control
Association. Website: http://www.isaca.org.

OGC's IT Infrastructure Library (ITIL) best practices.
Website: http://www.itil.co.uk.

The Capability Maturity Models from the Software Engineering Institute
at Carnegie Mellon University. Website: http://www.sei.cmu.edu.

The European Foundation for Quality Management (EFQM) and the
"Plan-Do-Check-Act" model is incorporated into EFQM.
Website: http://www.efqm.org.

Annex E: Early Adopters of BS 15000

Barclays

BBC Technology Ltd.

BSI

Centrica

Cap Gemini Ernst and Young (CGEY)

Elsevier

GlaxoSmithKline

Marval Ltd.

NTL

Police IT Organisation (PITO)

Xansa

Yorkshire Building Society (YBS)

Index